THE TAYLOR TRADING TECHNIQUE

GEORGE DOUGLASS TAYLOR

TRADERS PRESS, INC
GREENVILLE, SC

ISBN 10: 0-934380-24-4
ISBN 13: 978-0-934380-24-9

Cover design and layout by Shelley Mitchell, editor.

Traders Press, Inc.
PO Box 6206
Greenville, SC 29606
www.traderspress.com

(800) 927-8222 • (864) 298-0222
customerservice@traderspress.com

Publisher's Foreword

I first learned of Taylor's "BOOK METHOD" in 1975, from a colleague's client who had traded commodity futures for over 40 years. At this time, I was early in my 22 year career as a futures broker. This trader, Charles Ballentine, to whom I dedicated my 1979 book, *The Trading Rule That Can Make You Rich**, was the most astute, knowledgeable, and "market-savvy" trader I met during my brokerage career. He considered the method described herein as one of his most valuable tools as a short term trader. The "dog-eared" and coffee-stained copy of the book that I obtained from him was the only one I was able to obtain for many years to come, as it was out of print and virtually impossible to find.

In more recent years, this method has been re-popularized by George Angell in his books: *Winning in the Futures Market* and *How to Triple Your Money in Stock Index Futures Every Year,* in which he retitled it the *LSS Method.* Linda Bradford Raschke, one of the "New Market Wizards" uses Taylor's methodology extensively in short term trading and has highly recommended this book during her speaking engagements.

Since Taylor was similar to the legendary W. D. Gann in that he appears to have been a far better trader than writer, this book is NOT easy reading. In order to facilitate an easier understanding of this material, I am reprinting comments from Linda Bradford Raschke on how to use this method published in the *Club 3000 News,* and George Angell's 40-page section on Taylor's technique in his *Winning in the Futures Market.* Though placed at the back of the book, the reader may find it easier to understand Taylor's writing if Raschke's and Angell's comments are read first.

Edward Dobson

Edward D. Dobson, President
Traders Press, Inc.®

Preface

In preparing this work the author has felt the difficulty which arises in a theoretical dissertation on so practical a subject as speculation.

While trying to describe the action around one kind of trading objective, it is, also, necessary to try to describe the nearby future 'play' at the same time, since, the entire method is anticipatory and forecast.

This accounts for much of the repetition for in trying to describe the action around a Buying Point, for instance, we must, also, try to describe the action that precedes and leads up to this point, what action, should it occur, it forecasts for the next nearby future move.

Though theory and practice are not at variance when combined, yet either without the other proves very unsatisfactory. Thus, the reader should he start with only the theory, will find himself for some time pretty much "at sea" when he comes to actual practice.

As, however, he gradually obtains some practical experience, he may find this method of trading some use to him. So, also, the seasoned trader, who before, entrusted to luck, keenness of observation, intuition and experience, may find himself in the future much better equipped by acquiring a little theory.

While the statements in the work are predicated upon fundamentals, no reader should accept them as hard and fast rules, without exceptions. Statements that have been made are based on a long period of observations of what generally takes place, around these objectives but a trader must not be so rigid as to stick to a stubborn theory. Successful speculation is not based on any one set of inflexible rules and a trader must be ready to change when conditions change, however, the trader who knows how to act when the expected happens, is in a better position to act when the unexpected happens.

We have included just as much material as we think would be interesting and useful, saving a lot of time and the trouble of wading through a vast amount of superfluous and irrelevant matter, so far as trading with this method is concerned.

George Douglass Taylor

Table of Contents

Part I: *The Taylor Trading Technique*

Part II: Additional Material

Part III: Supplementary Articles

THE TAYLOR TRADING TECHNIQUE

CHAPTER 1
HOW THE MARKET TREND IS MADE

The "TAYLOR TRADING TECHNIQUE" [is] a book kept in tabular form to anticipate and follow the trend of prices as they appear on the 'tape' and to point out the important, stopping places, for buying and selling, wholly concerned with the technical side of the market for trading in grains, stocks and other commodities.

The BOOK Method is particularly adapted to the daily trading in grains—for normally there is more activity and it does not require so great an investment—and to the daily trader who aims to profit by the rise and fall of the daily movements and who trades in from One to Twenty Thousand Bushels or the price equivalent in stocks. These are not limits but about the average trading orders.

The trader who uses the short term method does not need to look very far ahead, therefore, the Book Method, does not concern itself with commodity economics nor speculation in [its] broader sense nor does it require the keeping of daily charts—it is not a charting system—the reading of or dependence on daily telegrams, weather reports, open interest and the mass of other market comment put out each day.

It is concerned entirely with Objective Points for Buying, Selling and Short Selling one the Minor Movements of the market and in training a trader to depend upon his own judgment and from his book he can and will get his own 'tips' on the movement of prices and in advance of any of the published 'chatter' provided each day for the traders and he can depend upon them and

move with greater assurance and safety than on the daily 'dope' he reads.

The trader does not reach for the gossip file when he comes in, his decision has been reached before the market opening—he is ready to trade or not to trade—at the opening or shortly after—unencumbered by comments or opinions from any source.

Of course, a trader should study and know all about his business the same as in any other line of endeavor but he must not permit any outside influence to interfere with these Objective Points as they appear on the tape, for he will find that, as they appear and pass that they will have discounted all the nearby news, and he must not and cannot ignore the prices as printed on the tape, and these prices will appear contrary most of the time to the news he has just read in the 'daily dope sheets' around the board room.

A Grain-Stock Trader, Operator, is exactly what a speculator should be, an operator, manipulator and a trader and he must understand the fundamentals of manipulation to be a good trader since manipulation enters into the market at all times.

In other words a good manipulator would be a good trader but it does not follow that a good trader would be a good manipulator, however, they would both be well versed in the manner of how buying and selling moves prices in the markets.

Before organized buying or selling, that is, pools, were prohibited a manipulator working with a stock or commodity would be compelled to trade in thousands of shares or bushels, as the case may be in the course of putting up the price and much of this trading was for his own account, in order to make money for himself, in addition to the accumulated commodity he hoped to sell at higher prices for his associates, however, with all the prohibitions the action of the market then and now, is just about the same in [its] movements. Prices still continue to move up and down at regular intervals when individuals are independently working towards the same end.

Now suppose the speculator that understood the fundamentals of manipulation wanted to do some trading, what would he look for, well, he would first look for inside buying or selling and since this is all revealed by the tape, this is just what he would do—he would read the tape trying to discern the buying and selling and which way prices were moving or more apt to move, in other words the trend—The trader using this method would look for a movement more or less mechanical in [its] action for tactics of manipulation do take on a mechanical action after awhile and for the simple reason of the pattern prices form through repetition.

Let us look at the manipulative side of the market and what takes place preparatory to move in a stock or commodity and the tape action is the same for all, grains, stocks and commodities.

We will start with a stock during accumulation, for our trading we are not concerned with why it takes place nor for what purpose but we know that periods of congestion are for accumulation or distribution but what interests the BOOK TRADER at these times is the type of trading, the buying and selling, and the way it moves prices and it is at these times when the action becomes most mechanical as the book shows.

Now let us assume that all the preliminary work has been done, general and special information on a particular stock or commodity, together with all other information pertaining to crops, supply and demand, and earnings and business conditions on stocks, and you can be sure that these matters will be studied and analyzed before any concentrated buying or selling takes place—and this is why the BOOK TRADER need not pay, too much, attention to these matters—he knows that once a trend starts—Bull or Bear—that it will continue for an indefinite period of time and that either way it will contain many Trading Areas, rallies and declines.

Now accumulation of grains and other commodities are for the major part for purposes other than speculation, in fact only a small percent is for speculative purposes, however, this small percent does at times cause prices to move violently both up and down.

Let us assume that conditions are favorable and a move is about to start, demand from some source and for some purpose starts it—and here again the BOOK TRADER is only interested in [its] starting, the movement, and not much concerned with which way it goes—now what happens, well, some day on the tape you see that a particular stock or future has become quite strong and active with the price rising, now, you observe this action for a few days and you will see that it only goes up so far, stops, then starts down. It reacts a little, something seems to arrest the downward movement and then it starts up again but notice it goes up a few cents or points or more then it goes down a few cents or points more but if you analyze the movement from the time it starts from the bottom of the minor move up to the top of the minor move, you will notice that it required about three days on the average, while the corrective decline was completed in one or possibly two days.

Let us suppose this stock or future was being manipulated with the intent to put up the price, just how would it be done, well, one of the ways and perhaps a method employed by most manipulators both past and present would be for him to start buying, assuming of course that he already had accumulated his line and other conditions were right for a move.

He would FIRST start by buying all the stock or grain above the market, for some little distance, say, four or five cents or points or more —this stock is the resting orders of those traders that are 'hung up' and others that would like to get out of the market, relieves the market of that pressure, clearing the way for trading purposes and establishes the price trend as up. The buying of this stock would not take place, unless it was the intent to try to put the price higher.

By making the stock active, coupled with the rising prices, the traders, professionals and the buying public, attracted by this activity come in as buyers. This outside demand is filled with the stock the operator was compelled to buy in starting the move and the demand for the stock caused by this buying should be more than he was forced to accumulate in the earlier stages of the movement. When this happens he sells it short and this is just what the experienced trader reading the tape would do, he would notice the slackening of the rise and the fact that there was no inside buying and he would sell it and sell it short.

The market being deprived of the buying power in starting the move by those making the market plus the stock fed out from the inside, fills the demand by the traders and with this demand filled the stock ceases to advance.

The experienced traders noting the lack of buying orders and the slowing down or checking of the rise sell out and take their profits and they, also, sell the stock short. The weight of this selling starts the stock or future down and when this happens the operator starts to support it—he buys back from the traders the stock or grain he sold them a few cents or points above the market and he, also, covers the short sales he put out when the stock was in demand—This buying back of the long stock and the covering of the short stock checks the decline.

The operator then follows the same procedure all over again, he takes all the stock or grain offered on the way up and the price begins to rise a second time. He repeats this process of alternately buying and selling, he buys on the way down and sells on the way up but always working higher, he supports the stock at higher levels on the declines and this may be weekly or monthly. This procedure continues all the way up to the top of the rise, this buying and selling keeps the market in check and helps to stabilize it and the rise and fall of prices causes the trading market.

This is the reason why the book becomes mechanical in [its] recordings of the minor trends—it points out the Main Objectives on the respective trading days, even though, any one of these sessions may be filled with currents or cross-currents, smaller rallies and declines.

On the Buying Day Objective we expect support and we watch the tape to confirm this buying for support and for a rally to start.

On the Selling Day Objective we expect selling and we watch the tape for confirmation of this selling and a reaction to follow.

On a Short Sale Day Objective we expect a hesitant action of the rise and we watch the tape to see if the selling is stronger than the buying and if the buying is being overcome by the selling, in which case we expect a decline to start when the action slows down or stops.

Now we understand how a stock or future starts up when the move is on, then reacts, then starts up again and as the bottoms are edged higher the tops have to be broken to go higher. The bottoms are support levels, temporarily, and on the tape you will usually see a little trading around a point like this, the same when a stock gets up to the top of a minor move, a supply point, here again a little trading takes place. This is not always the case for at times the low will have been reached on the down side by each transaction dropping the price lower until it is supported.

At times when the way is clear and there are few or no selling orders for some little distance above the market, the operator will run the price up fast, this action creates interest among the traders and brings in buying, the stock of which in turn is supplied by the operator and gives him a chance to sell a little long stock and to put out some short sales.

With the Book Trading we are concerned, only, with the Objective Points and we don't care much whether the price goes straight up or down to reach them. Of course, when these Objective Points are reached by a little trading it gives the trader more opportunity to buy and sell and he can usually get better executions but, also, when the stock goes straight up or down to these Objective Points it is the strongest action for a quick and sure play.

The book trader just simply follows the trend of prices as they are recorded in his book and the book more or less records the rhythm of the market for Buying, Selling and Short Selling and once into this swing it records it in a very dependable manner.

It is a fact and the records show it, for many years back that the market has a definite 1-2-3 rhythm, varied at times with an extra beat of 1-2-3-1 and at times 5, these figures represent days. The market goes up 1-2-3 days and reacts, the 4th and 5th figure is the variation when it runs that extra day or two on the way up and on the way down in both Bull and Bear trends. This beat of the market subject to these occasional variations occur with surprising regularity, so it seems that the same methods of manipulation used in the past are still used today, that is of buying and then selling every third or fourth day in an uptrend and reversed for a downtrend and this action the book records very faithfully.

We consider 3 days as a trading cycle—the 4th and 5th days are the (1st) and (2nd) days of a new cycle. We use the 1st day for buying and the 2nd and 3rd days for selling. This holds true in our 3 Day Trading Method and has but one exception in our daily trading which is explained in the chapter—Buying Day Low Violation.

The Book Method of trading is based on this rhythm and repetitious movement in the market but the tabular form with [its] columns and rings around the highs and lows on the respective trading days, with the trend signals for Buying, Selling and Short Selling were devised and designed from observation and research over a number of past years.

To the Book trader each day is a complete cycle—he has an Objective that he anticipates, he is always looking for it, it means to him a Buying or Selling Point or a place at which to Sell Short.

There is no more asking anybody what they think of the market—for having read these pages up to this point, you can guess just about how much their opinions would be worth, unless they were greatly experienced traders and in that case they probably wouldn't have an opinion to offer,

"not so you could notice it"—it depends entirely on how the trader thinks and his experience and patience. The trader depends on his book and his book depends on him, by this is meant, that he must keep his daily entries correct, the openings, highs and lows and the closing prices and carefully enter and watch the trend signals, the (X) and (√)marks for they point out and keep him on the correct trend at all times.

The Book Method follows the average of about a one day reaction for a decline and at times, usually in a strong uptrend the decline low will be made in one session, the low will be made on the Short Sales Day, however, another decline will generally take place from this low and the testing of this low will come on the next day, on the Buying Day, at which time the decline will generally stop—at, a little above or slightly penetrate this low. When the price holds above this low on a Buying Day, we call it Buying a Higher Bottom.

We accept profits on a one day rally and this is the spread from the Buying Day Low to the High on the Selling Day.

We allow one day more of rally to exhaust the movement and put the stock or future in a position for a Short Sale.

We treat a Bull and Bear Market as one continuous trend and we trade all the up and down movements in a Rally or Decline Area with one exception, as will be explained in the chapter on trends.

In an Uptrend Trading Area, we know the tops and bottoms are progressively higher and we allow this one day more of rally, this is the move from the Selling Day low to or through the Selling Day high on a Short Sale Day, we allow this one more day of rally to exhaust the swing upward—for a Short Sale.

In the Downtrend Trading Area, we know the tops and bottoms are progressively lower and we allow this one day more to exhaust the down swing to buy on. This buying 'spot' is explained under the chapter of Buying on a Buy Day Low Violation.

The trader using the Book Method must do his trading 'at the market' never limit an order nor use 'stops' and he must not expect to get tops or bottoms but it is surprising how many times he will get them after a little experience and even to the last eighth. After a little experience and practice he will begin to get that 'feel' of putting in his order at exactly the right time.

This is the kind of mood a trader should be in, not worrying because he did not get the extreme of either play, he needs to 'feel' he is right when he makes his play and when it turns out just as he anticipates it will, he has an intangible far greater than the material gain and there is no profit that gives greater satisfaction to a trader than the one he makes by being right.

He will find that after a little study of the Decline and Rally Columns in his book that he can gauge and average the spreads, from lows to highs and highs to lows, as the stock or future moves along, and can see his Objective, in a certain range as the stock or future starts to move and in the earlier stages, and will see the prices swing wider as the future gets further into the delivery month, and near the expiration date, and as stocks get away from their bottoms and into higher ground.

He has these columns to show him the spread from the narrowest move to the widest move, from a rally to a decline and from a decline to a rally and, also, his rules that point out the Buying and Selling Objectives automatically.

In the beginning or early stages of a move and in periods of congestion, accumulation or distribution, his Objective Points will just be about reached and exceeded by small fractions, they just about penetrate on both rallies and declines but as the movement opens up and becomes active, he must not be too anxious to buy or sell, he must hold himself in check, for as a trader develops and learns and begins to anticipate the moves, he will find that he must tone down his courage and the impulse to make a trade too soon.

Right here it must be pointed out that the Grain Market is a fast mover when it gets going but the Trader's Book, is faster than the market, it is always anticipating the future trade, as is the trader. He knows what to look for and expect, therefore, he must allow the market time to trade a little when his Objective Points are near

or slightly exceeded for after the future gets swinging he will find that his Objectives, will not only be reached and passed but will run through for much deeper penetrations than in the earlier stages of the movement and these are the real profit making plays.

NEVER MAKE A TRADE UNLESS IT FAVORS YOUR PLAY

If you can't 'feel' or see a profit in the market or if the spread is, too narrow, between the Objective Points, wait for a more favorable position, for a study of the summaries of the past expired grain futures and stocks, will show the great number of trading opportunities and how frequently they come along—by this is meant that—the Objective Points—will be made FIRST 'X' or LAST 'Y' and the correct determination of these signal marks reveal the Real Trading Trend and show it as weak or strong in the direction it is moving.

If your Objective is to Buy or Sell, wait, for the Buying or Selling Objective, don't be tempted to sell short just because the market looks so strong —for you will probably be making a trade on a strong cross current and against the Real Trend.

Many times when we are expecting a decline and 'feel' sure the stock or future will decline, the price will hold tight near the top and use up most of the trading session in doing it, only to 'roll over' and decline near the close. The same with a rally, the stock or future will trade most of the session near the low, then rally near the close. Don't be impatient because the market, temporarily, seems to be going contrary to your Objective.

The Objective Point when made FIRST— on a Buying, Selling or Short Sale Day, is the strongest and nearly always results in a quick profitable trade.

The Real Trend of the market is the trend between these Objective Points and this is the trend we try to buy and sell on, as distinguished from the many currents and cross-currents, small rallies and declines, first one way and then a reversal and then a swing back to the trend, before this deviation—towards the Buying or

Selling Objective. These smaller currents only confuse and do not change the course of the ultimate direction towards the Buying or Selling Objectives.

The uniformed trader buys into the market more because it is on a reaction or a low point and by luck he hits the real trend just as the stock starts to rally, then he sells out with a few points profit but on his next trade, he buys or sells on one of these cross currents and the trade promptly shows him a loss not only of his recently won gains but it takes a 'bite' out of his capital and after a few trades of this kind he has a losing average.

The Book Trader takes losses, of course, but he knows why and realizes that by so doing he is playing for position and a more profitable opportunity that he knows will come along and without much delay and when to expect it and how to capitalize on it.

The Book Trader knows that, even though, he may have an advantage with his method of trading that he does not have a sure-fire means of operating in the market and—it is well that no such method has been devised—that he must treat his trading as a full time job, yet, he knows that he can win on balance and this is about all that can be expected from trading or any other hard thought out business proposition. The trader by studying his book sees that the entire business of trading is an average—and this is true even for the insider—but on the winning side.

All his plays are an even break that he will make a profit, much greater when he wins, than the loss when he loses. Any method or system that gives you a 50-50 chance is a pretty good one with all [its] faults.

A check and study reveals the fact that the market repeats the same action (50%) of the time, in other words, that the penetration of a Sale Day High will occur 50% or better out of the total Selling Day High Objectives. The same with a Short Sale or a Buying Day Objective. The failures to penetrate these Objectives, also, preserve this same movement.

That these trading Objectives will occur, just as he expects them to do, is a reasonable probability and that he can trade at a price that will show him a profit and that in the longer term of trading the average will be in his favor.

A great amount of research has been devoted to this action with the results, that over a long period of time, stocks and all grain futures have shown the same pattern of movements with little or no variation, so it is reasonable to suppose, that the action in the future will continue to follow this same pattern of the past

There is enough similarity in the actions of all stocks and grains to warrant classifying them altogether for this average of recurrence or 'repeats' on the rallies and declines, however true, this may be of their actions as a whole, some stocks and grain futures while preserving the same movements will swing wider on the rallies and declines and will make their highs and lows at different times but the trader who keeps a book on the movements of a half dozen or so stocks and grains will be able to 'spot' the active wide swinging ones and confine his trading to them.

We separate and designate each trading day for [its] own expected action and we eliminate from our minds all other actions and influences about us, we concentrate on the stock or future we are trading in at the time, we try to remember, only, that action which can take place or happen around the particular Objective Point that we intend to trade on, as a Buy, Sale or Short Sale Day.

We don't listen to the 'gossip' nor what the news on the ticker happens to be at the moment nor do we pay any attention to the telegrams of what 'they' in Chicago are doing, the results will appear on the 'tape' and before their publication.

On a Buying Day, for example:—We observe the number of points the stock is down from the high—Short Sale Day—we notice whether the stock or grain opened up and continued a little higher and is making the high FIRST or whether the stock opened down and is declining further, making the low FIRST. Making the high FIRST we look for selling at this point and a reaction to follow. Making the low FIRST we look for support buying and a rally to follow. We notice if the price sold under the previous day and how much. We know the average the decline can sell down, under at this point and we compare this decline to see if it is average, above or below and we note the activity and kind of trading at this point.

Making the high FIRST we look for selling here above the—Short Sale Day High—a reaction usually starts from here and we observe whether the stock 'sold off easy' or whether the decline is stubborn and whether each transaction decline is meeting with support, that is, being taken easily or the buying is backing away and if the price is holding above the previous low—Short Sale Day Low.

We notice if the stock seems to be sort of 'bouncy' above this low, a decline being made on this kind of action usually bounces back a little after the low point is made and considerable trading takes place above it. From here the rally can and often does start with each transaction decline falling short of the low, in other words, the stock begins to hold these small gains. From this action we look for and expect a strong closing and it shows the real trend as up and this is the trend we trade on. How and when to buy is covered under the Buying Day chapter.

The above is pointed out as parts of 'tape' reading and you can believe the tape at all times, learn to read it and believe in nothing else for short term trading.

Tape reading is difficult and requires long experience and an understanding of the fundamentals of speculation and the market but the real heart of 'reading the tape' is to be able to detect concentrated buying and selling and to determine the trend of prices. Observation and memory, coupled with mental arithmetic of percentages. You have got to remember what you see and your calculations are made instantly, not with a pad and pencil but with your head.

Fortunately the minor movement with [its] habit of repeating so regularly has given us these Objective Points, so called, which point out places around which we may expect this concentrated buying and selling, eliminating a lot of hard work, that of watching each transaction on the tape and the book keeps these

Objectives in a more or less automatic way for us which further lessens the strain,—at above or below these Objectives we expect buying or selling and knowing about where to look for it. We eliminate all the smaller trends in between any two of these Objective Points.

On a Short Sale Day, for example:

From a low on a Buying Day, there will be thousands of transactions on the tape, in between and before the price reaches the Short Sale Day Objective—three sessions in the future —assuming the rally from a Buying Day low to the Short Sale Day High, is one of the many times a stock or future makes a move of this kind—A strong close on a Buying Day, a high made FIRST with a penetration of the selling Day Objective, then a reaction and a strong close, with an Up opening and a high made FIRST with a penetration of the Short Sale Day Objective—the Sale Day high. See (RZ) Chart for October 13,14,15.

This action is about 50% of the time, usually in an Uptrend Trading Area, in the Seasonal upswing. This is the longest unbroken rally the minor trend can make, for if it closes on the high of Short Sale Day and opens up on the following day—the Buy Day—it would be starting another cycle and at another point at which we can, also, make a trade. We would not put out a short sale when the high was being made LAST on a Short Sale Day. We would wait for the high made FIRST on the Buying Day—it would be starting another cycle and at another point at which we can, also, make a trade.

We are assuming here that the stock rallied on one of these unbroken swings, as in the above case and we are, Now, at the Short Sale Objective.

Our Short Sale is made at or through the previous high and this would be the high of Selling Day—We have our average of Short Sale Exceeded Points in the column in our book —now just as the high is about to be penetrated we observe the kind of trading that takes place, the stock may trade through this point in an 'easy' manner and apparently seem in 'no hurry' this kind of action takes the price through for a little deeper penetration before it reacts, but also, the penetration may be made by one or a few 'jerky' transactions and in fractions of a point, the stock seems to be in a hurry reaching up for 'something' before it reacts. The decline here is usually rapid on the down side. The price generally breaks fast from a top of this kind. This action is further explained under the chapter—A Short Sale Day.

The trader using the Book Method of trading has a choice, in that he has an Objective for each trading day or he can use the Three Day Method, that of buying and then selling every third day.

This Three Day Method is explained in a later Chapter.

CHAPTER 2
HOW TO MAKE UP THE BOOK

To make up a book we first head-line it with the yearly date above the first column, then put in the name of the stock or commodity, then in the first column put in the month, starting day and date.

The next four columns are for the entries of the daily prices, the Opening, High, Low and Close.

These entries are made daily for a period of about Ten (10) Days or Three (3) Swings, then go back and ring them with a circle, taking the lowest price reached in this period, the first cycle will be in the third column and this low point we designate as a Buying Day. The high of the day before in the second column, ring and make it a Short Sale Day, the high going back one more day, ring and make it a Selling Day. Then continue this circling in the same order back to the starting day of the book. Now coming back to the Buying Day Low—195 7/8—we carry forward in the same order. We have a book that reads; A Buying Day, A Selling Day, A Short Sell Day, then, A Buying Day, A Selling Day, and a Short Sell Day, etc.

We are not concerned with how the book started on the first day, whether it was a Buy, Sell or Short Sale.

The book is always kept in this order, never change the continuity and there are no lines left open for Sundays or Holidays, the market is considered as a series of continuous sessions without a break.

The Single page Plate on the next page shows how a trader would make up a book starting from any date, in the market and continuing forward.

This cut is the actual size of the 'Book' the trader carries with him and all information and records he will need in his work will be contained within it. (Next Page, page 17) These books can be bought at all stationary stores and come horizontally ruled, so that all the trader need do is to draw in the lines forming the columns, then head-it up. Two grain options or stocks can be kept in each book. The cut shows how the 'BOOK' will appear when made up. Observe the markings.

This page shows the trading carried back (18) days and the two pages together give a broader picture of the movement.

These reproduced pages show nearly the 'whole of the movement' the highs and lows made FIRST and Last, in series and mixed, the penetrations made FIRST and Last and the failures to penetrate the Objectives, Buying Day Lows Under, Higher Buying Day Bottoms, and Buying Day Low Violations. The possibilities of the Three Day Trading Method, the long side, only, or the long and short side combined.

This movement is part of an Uptrend Trading Area—notice the closing price on June 9th and on July 21st—a gain of (95/8) Cents—observe the units in the 'D' and 'R' Columns in order to accomplish this gain.

It is not claimed that a trader would get all these points but those he did get would be in cash and not on paper during all this trading time and his only commitments would be his purchases—a short sale covered and a buy 'long', on July 21st. The 'long pull' trader assuming he held on through all these ups and downs would still be confronted with the question of when to sell in order to get some part of these (9 5/8) profit points.

The column marked 'D' is for a decline or the spread from a Short Sale Day high to the Low on a Buying Day and shows the number of points the price sold down, if there are no loss in points, we put in a Zero.

The small diagonal '\' mark placed above the unit in the 'R' rally column is used only where the Selling Day High exceeded the High of the day before—this is the High of the Buying Day.

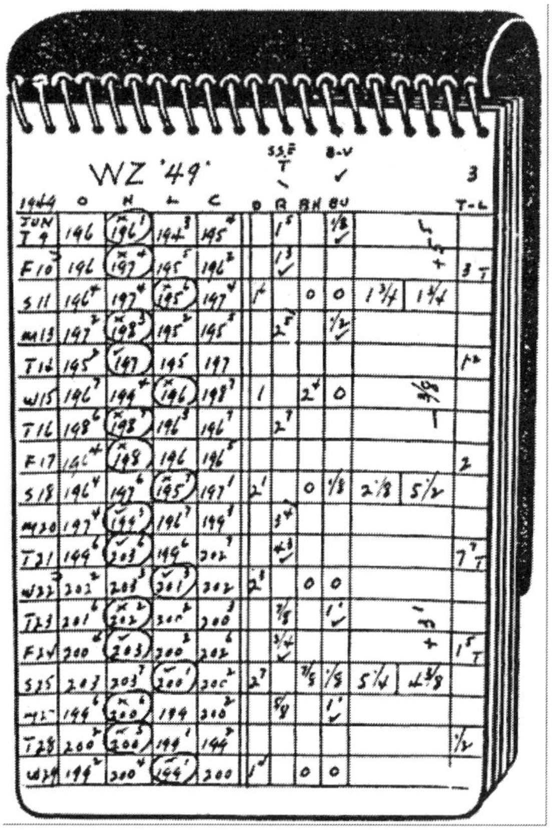

FIGURE 1

In this same column on the Short Sale Day line, we put in the number of points the Short Sale Exceeded the Selling Day High, otherwise there is no entry. For ready reference and for summation purposes, these entries can be alternated with different color inks.

The column marked 'BH' means a Buying Day High or the highest point at which it sold on a Buying Day and the number of points it sold through the Short Sale Day High Point, if it did not sell above this point, we put in a Zero.

The column marked 'BU' means Buy Under and shows the number of points on a Buying Day that the price sold under the low of previous day—Short Sale Day—if it did not sell under,

we put in a Zero.

The 'BU' column is, also, used for the 'BV' meaning Buying Day Low Violation, we put in the unit with a check under it when not using an ink of a different color. This column shows the number of points the price went lower than the Buying Day Low. We make this entry only when there is a violation.

The wide column is separated on the last day of the week and the square to the left is the total of the daily declines of the 'D' column and the square to the right is the total of the daily rallies of the 'R' column.

The figures running vertically are the loss or gain points from Saturday to Saturday closing prices. The number of trading points of the rallies and declines can be compared with the gain or loss points at the close of each week.

We do not keep a column of gains or losses of the daily closing prices for all our interests are centered in the spreads from highs to lows and lows to highs during each trading day. We are not concerned with a gain or loss at the close of the market.

The last column is used for the Three Day Method.

The last column, shows the spread or number of points from a Buying Day Low Point to the Short Sale Day High Point, in points gained and the 'T' means that it exceeded or sold through the Selling Day High. We put in the number of points and the 'T' beside it.

We have two marks (X) and (↲) and these marks point the trend of prices and are the most important signal marks.

The (X) means that the Objective for Buying, Selling or Short Selling was made FIRST.

The (↲) means that they were made LAST.

These marks are placed inside the Circles on a Buying, Selling and Short Sale Day, at the close if the session and show whether the high or low of the day was made FIRST or LAST.

We keep the highs and lows of the intermediate swings by drawing a line along side of the date column and mark it at each end with an arrow-head, between these highs and lows are our Trading Areas. Mark this line Up and Down using Blue and Red Inks.

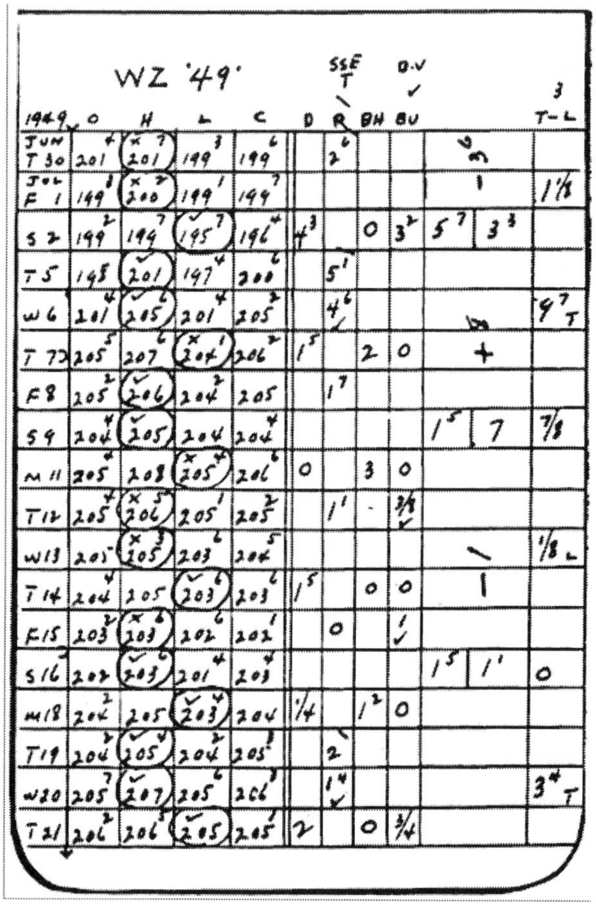

1949	O	H	L	C	D	R	BH	BU			T-L
WZ '49'					SSE T	D.V ✓					3
JUN T 30	201	201	199	199		2				3	
JUL F 1	199	200	199	199						1	1 7/8
S 2	199	199	195	196	4		0	3	5	3	
T 5	148	201	197	200	5						
W 6	201	205	201	205	4						9 T
T 7	205	207	204	206	1	2	0	+			
F 8	205	206	204	205	1						
S 9	204	205	204	204				1	7		7/8
M 11	205	208	205	206	0	3	0				
T 12	205	206	205	205	1	-	3/4				
W 13	201	205	203	204							1/8 L
T 14	204	205	203	203	1	0	0	1			
F 15	203	203	202	202	0		1				
S 16	202	203	201	203				1	1		0
M 18	204	205	203	204	1/4	1	0				
T 19	204	205	204	205	2						
W 20	205	207	205	206	1						3 T
T 21	206	206	205	205	2	0	3/4				

FIGURE 2

This page is from the actual transaction of the December Wheat Future, during this period. The Book' on (WZ) was started from the low price, a Buying Day, January 14th, the lowest price reached (10) days after the start of trading.

Chapter 3

Uses for the Columns and Marks

(The D Column - Decline Column)

The 'D' column shows the least and greatest declines from the high—Short Sale Objective—to the low—Buying Day Objective—in points and we use this column to get an average in order to judge this decline when it occurs. We have the records of the past and can note the greatest declines that have occurred and from this we can see just what might be expected at any time in the future.

We get the number of Short Sale opportunities and total of Short Sale points from this column.

Comparatively low priced markets work in a certain narrow range, the spread is narrow, comparatively high priced markets, of course, work in a wider range, the spread is wider, also, in the nearest future and near the expiration dates, the technical position at times causes wide spreads and with stocks after a long upward move with high prices.

The declines in this column are not always from true highs but we are not concerned with true or false highs but with the spread from a Short Sale Day High to the low on a Buying Day.

This column points out the number of buying opportunities in any one week and during the life of a grain option and with stocks they go on until the spread is too narrow to trade in them.

Generally the average of this column of declines points out the stopping places for buying 'Long' stock but the trading rule is a better check on the buying point and is summed up in the rule: "Cover Short Sales and Buy, at or below the low of the previous day on a Buying Day."

THE REASON FOR THE DECLINE ZERO

The amount of Rally from a Short Sale Day low, with the closing price up or on the high for the day, plus a wide up opening on the Buying Day. This Decline Zero does not happen so very often but it can be anticipated by watching the low of Buying Day and the high of Short Sale Day, when the low holds at the same or a higher price we can visualize the Zero in the 'D' column and a Decline Zero generally means nearby higher prices for a day and many times longer. See the WK and CK Plates and note the trend after a Zero appears.

We always cover the Short Sale on the same day when the spread is wide and or within the limits of about what a decline, normally, should be or has been, from the Short Sale Day High to the Buying Day Low. We see this range between the high and low and reason that if it does not go any lower, we see this low as our point at which to buy, next day, on our Buying Day.

We don't wait for the Buying Day on which to cover our Short Sale when the action is fast and 'panicky' and the 'sell off' in one session is within the range or more, the spread from Short Sale High to Buy Day Low, for fast declines many times are followed by fast rallies.

We cover our Short Sale and wait. We don't buy Long stock on this low, either, for the reason that the stock may or may not rally from this low and we only buy Long stock on a Buying Day or the Violation of a Buying Day Low made FIRST.

The stock from this low can do one or the other, close near the low without a rally or rally from this low and recover all the loss of the day and more. We don't care what it does for the balance of the session, we sold it short and covered with a profit but had we gone 'long' at this low and there were normally, we would be in a bad way, for the trend would be indicating further declines and we never make a trade unless it favors our play.

What we do after covering our Short Sale, is to wait for the next day where we watch this low and try to buy at or below it on our Buying Day.

Now suppose the stock did rally and closed up near the top or even higher than the opening of the day and—this is the reason on an action of this kind why we covered our Short Sale on the break—this then would point the trend higher and our Short Sale Day Circle would have a check (√) in it, the high was made last.

From this action we could expect the opening to be up and the price to be higher than the Short Sale Day high and on a Buying Day. The high made LAST on a Short Sale Day, we would not sell it again on this last high for it would indicate a high to sell on, made FIRST on a Buying Day.

We covered our Short Sale on the same day and have protected our profits, anticipating a rally from this low, one that might hold and the possibilities that we might have to buy a Higher Bottom on a Buying Day. By making our play in this manner we are trading on the REAL trend and not on one of these daily cross-currents. Buying a higher Bottom on a Buying Day usually results in a profit and the decline Zero is always a higher bottom.

THE 'R' COLUMN - RALLY COLUMN

The 'R' column shows the least and greatest rally from a Buying Day Low to a selling Day High in points and shows how much of the decline has been recovered, all, part or none and from this forecast of the trend as up or down for the next day or so and sometimes longer. On the Yearly Plates, notice the 'R' column unit after a large 'D' column unit and the action for a day or so after.

The 'R' column shows the number of selling opportunities and the total of rally points on the 'Long' side of the market.

Comparatively low markets work in a narrow range and high markets in a wider range, so that in narrow markets the rallies many times just about reach and penetrate the Selling Objectives, the same on the declines, while higher markets run through for much deeper penetrations, either way.

THE DIAGONAL MARK (\)

We have the Diagonal Mark placed above the rally figures that show the number of Selling Day penetrations and we can tally them for the number of times or percentage of times we get these penetrations or 'sell thru' or the number of times they 'fall short' or fail to penetrate. By studying them we can get an average out of the total Selling Objectives and know about what to expect at this point for penetrations. Study the Plates and notice how they penetrate at about the same fractions or points with occasional very deep penetrations, which when this happens is in the traders favor.

We find the average in grain futures of the recent past years was (56%) penetrations on the Selling Objective. These penetrations are almost sure profits, you can see the probable profit in the spread from the low to the high on the Buying Day, at the close of the market, plus the amount of penetration on the Selling Day of this Buying Day High.

Generally the trading rule covers our Selling Objectives: "Sell your Long stock at or through the high of the previous day, this high of previous day is the high reached on the BUYING DAY".

THE REASON FOR THE RALLY ZERO

The lack of rally from a Buying Day Low with a more or less 'flat' closing or on the low for the day, plus a wide down opening on the Selling Day. This Rally Zero does not happen so very often but it can be anticipated by watching the low on Buying Day and high on Selling Day, when the price holds at or under the Buy Day low we can visualize the Zero in the Rally column and the Rally Zero, generally means nearby lower prices. Also, see the Plates on this. The Rally Zero is a Buy Day Violation and the violation takes place on the opening, however, the low is usually made FIRST and generally a rally starts from this low. If the opening is not too severe, the rally many times comes up to and through the Buy Day Low and then starts to decline again from around this point. Many times it fails to reach it and at other times the rally will carry back and penetrate the Buy Day High. When buying on a Buying Day Low Violation, that is why we use the Buying Day Low as our Selling Objective, instead of the Buying Day High. Any fast come back through the Buying Day Low and then on up for a penetration of the Buying Day High is just that much more in favor of the trader who goes Long on this Violation.

After having bought at or near the low on a Buying Day Low and generally this occurs at the opening on the Selling Day. We sell and 'at the market' on any rally from this decline, should this low be violated, at this point we either have a small loss or a small profit. The profit when made is due to the rally that carries up through the Buy Day Low. The price sells lower than the Buy Day Low and then it generally rallies, not always, for the market can keep going down from here—this is why we get out as fast as we can on any rally from this low—generally this rally carries up to and through the Buy Day Low Point. We sell at or through this point always. Never hold on and hope for more rally, sell out here for what you can get. Big declines can start from here for this could be the continuation of a decline that had started from the High of Buying Day made FIRST and particularly so, if the stock or future is well into the upswing and prices are high.

When the unit in the 'D' column is large, the Buying Day, we act immediately upon seeing the price go lower than the Buying Day Low and generally this occurs at the opening on the Selling Day. We sell and 'at the market' on any rally from this decline, should this low be violated, at this point we either have a small loss or a small profit. The profit when rally unit in the 'R' column is generally small, there are exceptions but generally this is the case. In a panicky, severe 'sell down' at times the whole decline and more is recovered. This happens more often when some favorable news is announced during the trading session and the market technically is in a position to act on it, the market is oversold and

the fast rally is caused by short covering.

THE 'R' COLUMN FOR (SSE) SALE DAY HIGH EXCEEDED

The 'R' column is, also, used for the Short Sale Exceeded, meaning the Short Sale Day High exceeded or sold through the high of Selling Day. We enter this unit only when it 'sells thru' and from these entries we can get an average of about what to expect in the way of penetrations at this point and an average of how often it repeats this movement during the life of a grain future or during the longer term swing in a stock.

Recent past expired futures in all grains show that the Sale Day High was penetrated over (50%) of the time before the future expired.

These penetrations run from fractions to points but we can judge them by the price range of the stock, whether it is high, low, or at some point in between. News items at times cause deeper penetrations and the beginning of a rally from the low point reached in a Downward Trading Area.

This unit is put in on the same line as the Short Sale Day Circle and since it is under the rally or Selling Day unit it might be well to use different color ink to separate each of these units in order to avoid confusion in tabulation.

By studying this penetration and knowing where to look for a hesitating action you will be able to see, at times, the selling that is taking place at this point.

This is a place at which you can do a little 'tape reading' for knowing what to expect and at which point to look for it, you can check it easier to see if your expectations are coming true.

THE (BH) BUY DAY HIGH COLUMN

The BH column shows the number of times and the extent of penetrations of the Short Sale Day High, when there are no penetrations we put in a Zero. The (BH) and (BU) Zeros don't have the same forecasting significance as the Decline and Rally Zeros, however, the (BH) Zero when it appears does show the break and termination of the three day swing and establishes the high on the Short Sale Day.

We watch these penetrations and from them we can get an average of about what to expect at this point in the way of a 'sell thru' and we can tabulate them for an average or percent times they penetrate or fail to go through. This penetration is the place for a quick Short Sale when the price goes thru FIRST. In order to make this point FIRST, means that the rally must have started on a Short Sale Day and closed strong on this day, continuing to rally up to this point, making a two or more days of rally and generally this is enough to exhaust the minor swing and is in a position for a decline, of some extent.

At this point you can test your tape reading, the rally seems to be in an upward dead center and just about ready to roll over for a decline, generally this is the action at this point. This BH (Buy Day High) is generally made when preceded by a Buying Day Low Violation. This Buying Day Low Violation causes the decline to run one more day on the downside, therefore, the rally runs a day later on the upside. Generally the Short Sale Day High ends the (3) days swing, a violation delays it and causes the high to be made FIRST on the next Buying Day and with exceptions, this high still preserves the (3) day rally swing.

THE (BU) BUY UNDER COLUMN

The (BU) Column means, buy under, and shows the unit that the stock sold under the Short Sale Day Low, on a Buying Day, if there were no declines we put in a Zero. The (BU) Zero, points out the Higher Buying Day Bottoms and are all higher support levels, on the declines, from Short Sale Day rallies. The spread between these two points is the concession we try to buy at. We watch this column for an average and we see that it runs from fractions to points. Usually in an Uptrend Trading Area, the heaviest selling takes place on the Short Sale Day and the decline generally 'levels off' on the Buying Day—at, a little above or below, the low reached on the Short Sale Day.

Around this point is where we expect support

to come into the market and we watch the tape to confirm it. Support here would be inside short covering of stock sold on the last rally and the buying back of Long stock sold a little above the market to the outside traders. Those traders who buy at the top of rallies are buying the Long stock sold on balance and the short sales put out by the inside operators.

On the average trading day without inter-session news, in an Uptrend Trading Area (watch your trend line) the stock makes this low on the Short Sale Day and then trades around this point and closes fairly 'flat' and then opens down, the next day and sells a little under this low on a Buying Day, the decline just seems to 'level off' here and on this 'dip' is where we buy our Long stock. The low is made FIRST and usually a rally starts from here.

When the decline on a Short Sale Day is severe and the market is active, the stock makes a low and usually rallies fast and closes up nearer the high of the day, we can then expect a higher opening on the Buying Day and whatever reaction that takes place from this high falls short of the low made on the Short Sale Day and causes the (BU) Zero. The price then is being supported at a higher bottom and will generally start up again from this higher low point. The stock is then making a higher bottom and Buying a Higher Bottom is usually profitable.

THE (B V) COLUMN BUYING DAY LOW VIOLATION

The column marked (BU) is, also, used for the (BV) meaning Buying Day Low Violation and we enter this unit directly under the (BU) unit. This unit shows the spread of the decline, the amount it sold under the Buying Day Low point.

This decline we consider a 'false move' and when made FIRST it is usually recovered, even though, the market may sell down again after this rally. While it is part of a larger decline and begins to show up at the starting of a Down Trend Trading Area and continues through this area, it is profitable to trade on this kind of action most of the time. It takes place from a decline on a

Buying Day and where there was no rally and the close was heavy and usually right on the low of the day. This action indicates lower prices and we expect a down opening on the Selling Day and unless we are in a market of high prices from which Downward Limit Days could take place or Downward Secondary Reactions in stocks, it is, also, a 'leveling off' of a two or three days decline.

We watch for support at any place under the Buying Day Low—check back for two or three weeks for a recent range on these Violation declines, had they been fractions of a point—more or less—and the present price of the stock. When this decline low is made FIRST and early in the session, we buy as near this low point as we can.

At this point we are considering the everyday, average market movement, so called, surprise news and scares are treated in another chapter.

We are watching the market and we see the price under the Buying Day Low and we note that his low is being made FIRST and shortly after the opening and is under a couple of cents. For example:—We note this two cent decline plus the unit of decline in the 'D' column and the total then is Six (6) Cents, this is a considerable decline and normally would call for some, rally at this point. Now, we are buying on a Selling Day and where we usually watch the high of

Buying Day to be penetrated as our Selling Day Objective we now change on account of the Violation and make the low point of the Buying Day, our Selling Objective, for this Long stock we bought.

The market usually rallies from a Violation decline made FIRST and comes up to and through the Buying Day Low point. We bought and we now see the rally carry up to this low, at this point we can sell out with a sure profit. The stock has recovered all of this 'false move' and the market at this point can turn down again and does many times and it, also, at times continues up. Now in this latter case any further rally begins the percent recovery of the decline unit as shown in the 'D' column. In this case it is Four (4) Cents, now, each point of recovery is 25% of this decline and certainly after a rally that would recover the 'false move' or Violation points and 'wipe out' One Third to Two Thirds of the Real decline should be high enough for us, even though, it may rally too far, we 'cinch' our profits and begin to anticipate our next play for the chances are that on the next trade will be more room and profit and our next trade would be a Short Sale on the Short Sale Day High and would probably be made FIRST.

CHAPTER 4
THE SYMBOLS (X) AND (√) AS TREND INDICATORS

We have two marks (X) and (√) these marks point the trend of prices, they indicate the ending of or continuation of trends, depending upon the circle they are placed in and the kind of trading day.

The (X) mark means that the high or low was made LAST.

The (√) mark means that the high or low was made LAST.

These marks are placed in the circles on the Buying, Selling and Short Sales Days.

An example of the Objective being made FIRST:

As a supposition the stock reacted from Short Sales Day High and on the Buying Day made a low early in the season, then began to rally and traded the rest of the session between the high and low with the closing price nearer the high than the low. We would then put an (X) in the Buying Day Circle indicating the low as being made FIRST.

In a case of this kind and this is what the trader likes to see, the opening on the Selling Day would generally be up and with a penetration of the Buying Day High. The Selling Objective would be made FIRST and an (X) placed in this circle. The trader would sell—at or above this penetration of Buying Day High—and would be out of the market without much delay.

The stock having sold through the Selling Day FIRST there would generally be a reaction from this high, and even though the trader had sold out he continues to watch the low and close of Selling Day, for an indication, for the stock having reacted would again rally and close high enough to indicate an Up opening and another penetration of the Selling Day High made FIRST, this then would be on the Short Sale Day and the Short Sale Day Circle would be marked with an (X). On this penetration we would have a strong 'spot' for our Short Sale, since it was made

FIRST and usually a reaction would start from this point which would end again on our Buying Day with an (X) or (√) FIRST or LAST.

An example of the Objective being made LAST:

When the objective is made LAST the play consumes more time for the trader must watch the entire session in order to make a trade.

Suppose the stock had sold down from a Short Day High and made a low, then begun to rally and close Up from this low and at the opening was higher, making the high FIRST on a Buying Day then begun to 'sell off' all through the session and made a low, then began to rally and closed UP from this low and at the opening was higher, making the high FIRST on the Buying Day then began to 'sell off' all through the session and made a low but there was little or no spread from this low to the closing price. This then would be making the Buying Objective LAST and we would put a (√) check in the Buying Day Circle, this indicates the trend as down, at the close, even though it may be the end of the decline and is many times, but it also carries the implications of a Buying Day Low Violation.

Suppose the low was made FIRST on a Buying Day and the stock then began to rally from this low and closed up above this low but at the opening—Selling Day was off a little and traded down lower but did not break or violate the Buying Day low, then it began to rally and continued on up for the balance of the session and closed on the high of the day, this then would be making the high on Selling Day LAST.—We, of course, would sell our stock here on the penetration or failure to penetrate our Selling Objective— the Buy Day High—but it would require us to wait and watch the entire session in order to complete our trade.

On a Short Sale Day when the high looks like

it will be made LAST. We wait, never make a trade unless it favors your play. At this point we check back in our book for a Violation of the previous Buy Day low, if so, we expect the stock to continue up, even open up and make the high FIRST on the Buying Day and we watch for a Short Sale at this point, at or above the Short Sale Day High.

When the high is made FIRST on a Selling Day and the stock reacts and the reaction continues up to the market it will probably carry over to the next day, the low price would generally be made on the opening or after, then a rally would probably start that would carry the price up making the high LAST on a Short Sale Day but we do not put out short sales on a high made LAST.

When a stock or future completes [its] cycle from a Buy Day Low to a Short Sale High and all Objectives are made FIRST—and this is the kind of movement we like to see—See Plate on RZ 1943— you can see your profits as the movement unfolds.

During other of these cycles we get a mixed movement of the Objectives made FIRST and LAST and this is caused by the real trend being interrupted by the smaller rallies, and declines, currents and cross-currents that go on all through the trading session but in no way change the ultimate completion of our trading Objectives that is why we must at all times ferret out the Real trend and to be able to keep track of it, regardless of these inter-day 'Jiggles'. Our Book does this very thing for us, almost automatically by pointing out the kind of trading day and the signal marks show which way it is most likely to go.

Watch the results of some of the plays made by the traders that go counter to the specific trading days as shown in your book.

They buy and sell on rallies and declines during the day entirely ignorant of the kind of trend, at the time, they buy or sell. Once in a while if they trade often enough they will 'hit' the real trend and make a profit but the next trade will be nothing more than a guess and a wrong one at that with an ultimate total loss.

The import of the entire matter here, is that the insiders, operator or the force that is making the market go right along pushing towards the objective to the other are 'false moves' and they are the smaller trends that confuse the traders. That is why we must use the greatest of care in getting the signal marks correct—and this [is] difficult but the real trend follows these marks.

This example of a few years back shows part of the movement at a time when all Objectives were made FIRST—it shows one Buying Day Low at the low of previous day—Short Sale Day—on October 13th, and one Buy Day low—under—on Saturday 16th. It shows how the bottoms were just equaled and exceeded and how the tops were penetrated at the Selling and Short Sale Highs.

Prices during this period were in a narrow range of four or five points for a period of about nine weeks.

The 'D' and 'R' Columns total 8 1/8 points while the six days gain at the closing prices were 2 1/4 points—the trading opportunities were almost four times greater.

When the markets are narrow, the moves are small and the profits are small.

The recurrence of the Buy and Sell and Short Sale signals in series are not exceptions for the market is filled with them at times and the trading at these times is most mechanical as you can see.

The diagram shows two sets in series—a Short Sale, a Buy and a Sale—a Short Sale, a Buying and a Sale. All Made FIRST. At other times the series will be FIRST and LAST and Mixed.

When the series runs all signals made FIRST there is no delay, a trader buys and sells just as his Objectives are reached or penetrated. At other times when the market action is mixed the trader must watch the entire session in order to complete a trader and there will be sessions when it would be wiser to just stand aside and do nothing at all when the movement gets too narrow.

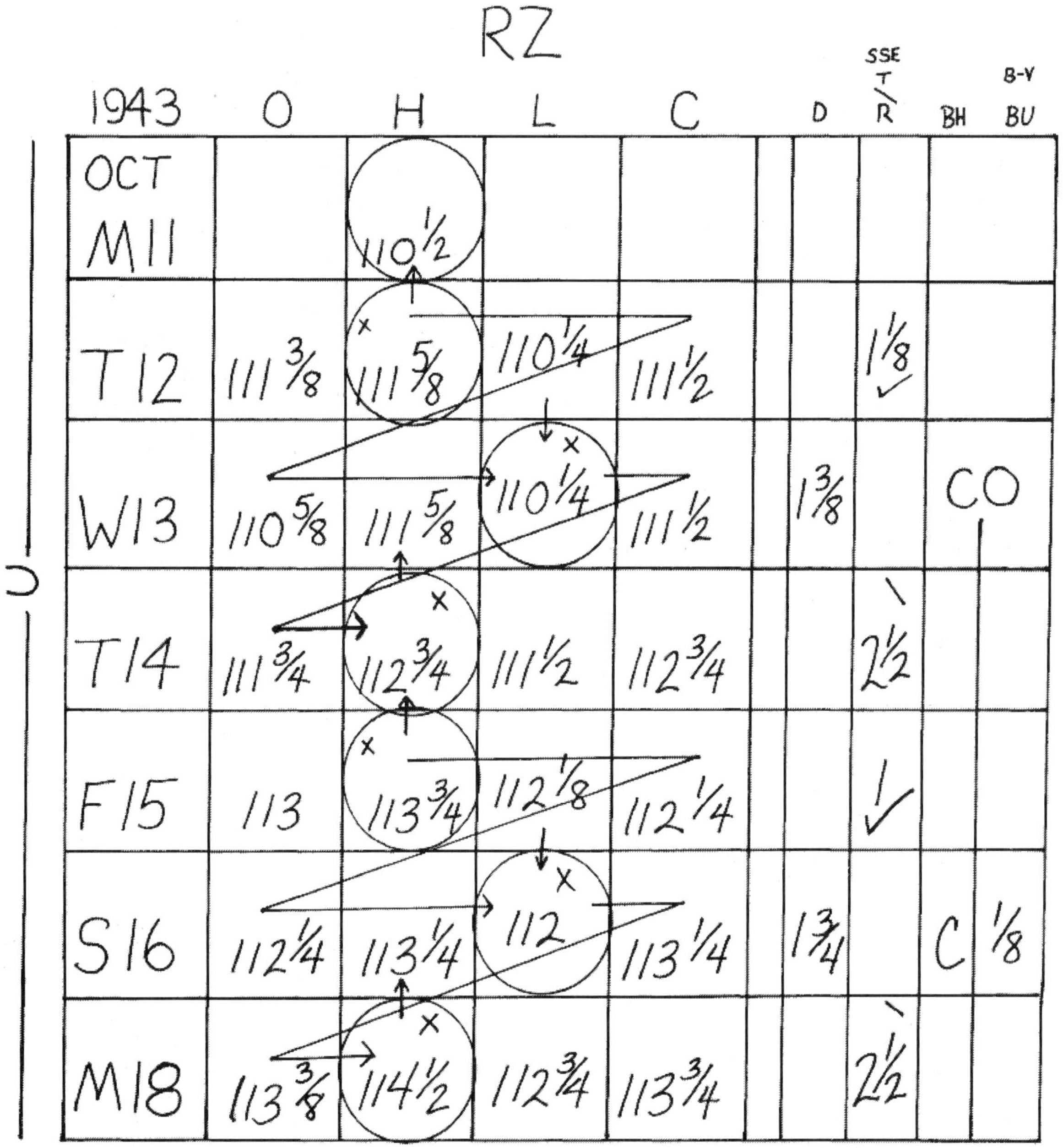

RZ

1943	O	H	L	C		D	SSE T/R	BH	B-V BU
OCT M11		110½							
T12	111⅜	111⅝	110¼	111½			1⅛ ✓		
W13	110⅝	111⅝	110¼	111½		1⅜			CO
T14	111¾	112¾	111½	112¾			2½		
F15	113	113¾	112⅛	112¼			✓		
S16	112¼	113¼	112	113¼		1¾		C	⅛
M18	113⅜	114½	112¾	113¾			2½		

FIGURE 3

CHAPTER 5
A BUYING DAY

We buy a stock or future when we think it is on a bottom dead center and the trend is just about to turn up and our selling is done on a top dead center when the trend is just about to turn down.

On a Buying Day when the stock rallies from the low and the gain in points is sufficiently large, we sell out on the same day. The rally may put the price up to and through the high of the day before—the Short Sale Day—and the close may be strong and the stock may even close on the high of the day, however, we sell out just before the close, for while strong or higher closing does indicate a higher opening and a continuance of the rally, this, should it happen, would only put the price through the Selling Day Objective, next day, so we don't take chances with this kind of a move and don't follow the rally too far, we secure our profits before the close of the market. An action of this kind is fast and the 'come back' rapid or the action may be quiet and slow with firm reaching up movement making new highs by fractions for several points and then end the move with a slight relaxation, then a smaller 'spurt' to reach the top or make a new high for the day, however, no matter how the high is reached it gives us our profit a day in advance of the Selling Objective by selling out before the close and we are not concerned with how high it may go on the next day.

The reason we sell out on the same day, is that the stock may open down and often does, from a run up of this kind or it may open at the previous close on the Selling Day and spend the whole Selling Day and not reach the Selling Day Objective—the Buying High—after which it can make one of two moves, close up with an indication that it will open up and sell through the top—Selling Day High—for a strong Short Sale Objective or close down near the low, an indication of failure to penetrate and a weak Short Sale Objective.

By selling out we have secured most of the long profits from a move of this kind and in many cases all of them and we got them without waiting for the Selling Objective—we are trading and take a 'lump sum' anytime the market gives it to us fast, even though, it may be a little less than we might get by waiting

Having 'sold out' and we are out of the market—on the Buying Day—we prefer to see this rally continue on the Selling Day for penetration of the Buying Day High, for we are now anticipating a future short sale and it would generally be strong short sale indication should the stock react from this penetration of Selling Day High for this short sale and it would be made after Three (3) Days of rallying.

On a Buying Day, we buy at, a little above or below the low of previous day—this would be the low reached on the Short Sale Day—we watch this range or spread on a Short Sale Day, the 'sell off' from high to low and at this low we can see, so far, the price we will have to pay, next day—The Buying Day—for our long stock provided the decline ends at or near this low but we can with reasonable certainty figure whether this low will be our buying 'spot' or if we may not expect further concessions to buy on and we get this indication from the way the stock closes on the Short Sale Day.

We get this indication by watching the close and whether prices are up or down, that is down from the high of day or up from the low of day, weak or strong. Remember, we are watching the prices on a Short Sale Day trying to anticipate the coming point at which we can buy or go 'long'—You will be short of the market on this day, too, but this action is covered under the chapter on a Short Selling Day. When the close is strong on a Short Sale Day, that is, the closing price is up from the low and nearer the high for the day, we expect a higher opening on a Buying

Day. When this happens, we wait for generally the price declines from a high made FIRST on a Buying Day.

The Short Sale Day Low is our point to watch and we watch for it to be reached or for the price to sell under this point, since this is where we buy our long stock.

In a strong uptrend the decline may 'fall short' of reaching this low and the rally on a Buying Day may start from a little above this low—this is what we call Buying a Higher Buying Day Bottom and generally it is profitable. The price may open up and rally farther, making the high FIRST, then starts to decline but the price on the decline gives way 'grudgingly' from each fractional 'sell off', the stock on the rallies seems resilient, it sort of springs back from each low. By watching the tape closely at this point, you can see and 'feel' the buying for support. In this case the Decline Column Unit is usually small.

We expect the price to fall short of this low, to stop a little above it when the trend is turning up from the low of a Trading Area, the bottoms have got to be progressively higher in an up-trend.

At a little above and below this point—the low of Short Sale Day—we watch for support and we note the range of prices around this level and the length of time the price trades in this range. By comparing the decline from the Short Sale Day High to the low as it is being made on the Buying Day, we can judge from the past declines of the 'D' column just what kind of a decline is taking place at the time and can follow it while it is happening, you can then note whether it is greater than average, less or about average—here again a small decline unit is followed by a larger rally unit in an Uptrend Trading Area.

Now, we go back to the close of the Short Sale Day and we find that it was a 'flat' closing, then from this indication we expect a lower opening on the Buying Day and so far this would cause the low to be made FIRST and is a stronger indication when made early in the session that a rally would start from this low and hold the gains for a strong closing, which in turn indicates an up opening and a penetration of the Selling Day Objective—the Buy Day High.

When the high is made FIRST on a Buying Day, this causes the low, our buying point to be made LAST and carries with it the possibilities that the stock may trade down with no indication to rally and the close may be near the low of the day, in which case we would not buy at all, even though it was lower than the low of Short Sale Day, for here we would anticipate and expect a Buying Day Low Violation and we would wait for it.

When the low of Buying Day is made LAST but is holding a higher bottom, that is the low is higher than the Short Sale Day Low, we buy as near this low as we can, for generally a rally starts from this higher bottom, however, should any gain at the close be lost on the opening of Selling Day and this decline may or may not cause a Buy Day Low Violation, we sell on any rally after this decline.

We use the Buy Day Low as our Selling Objective, we sell at the best price we can get above this low. The rally usually carries up to and through this low, even though it again declines. There are exceptions and times when it fails to reach this point and at such times it means a loss, then again, strong rallies at times not only sell up to and through this low but continue up to and through the High of Buying Day, completing the Primary Selling Objective with a penetration.

The low made on a Buying Day is the low and has nothing to do with whether it may be violated, the next day, you buy at what you consider to be the low and many times you will actually get it, allowing for the executions but after buying it may go a little lower but your line of thought changes after you have bought, even though, you did not get the last eighth, you now begin to watch any rally from the low, made by the stock—not the price you paid for it—you are now expecting the stock to rally and show a gain above this low, at the close, indicating a higher opening and a further uptrend, this shows your play is correct so far.

Even though, your profit will be a little less by reason of the price having sold down a little lower after you bought, the point to be made here is that, after having bought at what you considered the correct place, reverse your thinking about further declines or 'sell off' and begin to look forward to the place where you can sell out with a profit, in case of a rally this will be somewhere above the high of Buying Day, next day your Selling Day—unless the market hands it to you in the same session—the action we mentioned in the beginning of this chapter.

Suppose you bought at or near the low or right on the low and the stock rallied but began to sell down again and near the close lost all the gains, this then would be a 'flat' closing with the probabilities of the price going lower the next day.

A 'flat' or weak close on a Buying Day shows the short interest, inside or professional, in no great hurry to cover, therefore, an indication of a Buying Day Low Violation.

On an action of this kind, sell out before the close, for you are in wrong and you must not carry the stock into a greater loss, if you have a loss at this point by holding on and hoping for an up-opening on Selling Day.

After a low is made on a Buying Day and the stock begins to rally, it should hold a small part of the gains on each rally, each decline or set back should 'fall short' of the last low.

A trader takes losses, he must but he takes them when they are small, as in a case of having bought, then a rally, and then to see this gain lost, and the close at or slightly above the low of the day. He does not hold on and hope for a rally, he sells out before the close, takes this small loss and begins to anticipate buying a Buy Low Violation. Right here it is well to point out that up-openings do occur from 'flat' closings on any of our Objective Days, but in these cases it is some overnight news that can't be read on the tape before the close and we don't trade on what the market might do but try to trade on what it actually does and the probable future results. The trader by taking this small loss will generally get it back and with a profit besides on the next play or trade.

NEVER AVERAGE A LOSS, SELL OUT IF YOU THINK YOU ARE WRONG AND THEN BUY BACK AGAIN WHEN YOU BELIEVE

YOU ARE RIGHT.

The temptation at this point after having bought on the low or having the stock go lower after you have bought and then holding on when the stock opens down and sells down lower causing a Violation of the Buy Low, even though, the low is made FIRST is a strong 'spot' to make you want to average your loss and it looks like it would have been a 'cinch' after the rally sets in but Don't do it.

When prices are comparatively low and the Trading Area Trend is Up, a trader having bought at or near the low and to then see the stock close 'flat' need not worry, too much, for he can supplement his trade by using the (3) day method, he can hold on and generally sell his stock or grain at or through the high of—Selling Day—at a profit, however, in this case should the Buy Day Low be Violated the rally may be weak on account of this violation and fail to penetrate the Selling Day High on the Short Sale Day. The trader using the daily method of trading should stick to this method and be willing to take a small loss in order to better his position, rather than to switch to the (3) day method and then back to his daily method, for while he can save—at times—this small loss, it is bad medicine, especially if prices are very high for in the above case of the Violation—or any Violation—there may not be a rally—prices may continue on down. Trading this way might become a habit and a trader should use one or the other methods.

The trader who has been consistently using the (3) day method can stand a loss, even, if it is unusually large on account of his profits from previous plays—the summary of the yearly WK and CK show the loss day swings run about (12%) of the total and the gain days about (88%) however, occasionally a loss day swing can be very severe and the daily trader should not take chances where the loss could be greater than his greatest daily gain. The daily trader can trade on a 'shoe string' but the 3 day trader is prepared to finance himself over a 'bump' of this kind.

The daily trader must at all times be in complete command of his cash for use when he needs it, therefore, he takes small losses by selling out the instant he sees that he is wrong.

In the Uptrend Trading Areas, the low on a Buying Day is generally made FIRST with the closing price up from this low.

The 'flat' or weak closings are usually made in the Downtrend Areas.

Regardless of the kind of Trading Area—up or down—buying low points made FIRST on a Buying Day, are for the most part profitable— except in the precipitous decline after a steep downtrend gets under way.

Buying on a low point and then to see the price go a little lower does not prove you wrong, unless the price closes 'flat'—that is the low of the day and closing price is the same.

We do get up-openings from 'flat' closing but generally the little lower before the start of a rally.

Buying, too soon, only means that you need a little more in timing, in most cases.

Check the Yearly Plates on WK and CK on the Buying Days—for the times the price sold under the Short Sale Day Low—the times the Buying Day Low was Violated—also, the gain and loss day swings of the (3) day Column.

CHAPTER 6
BUYING ON A BUYING DAY LOW VIOLATION

The Buying Day Low Violation must be made FIRST and this would be the result of the Buying Day Low made LAST with a more or less 'flat' closing.

This action of a 'flat' closing favors the probabilities that the opening prices will be down and the opening is in itself often the start of the Violation and that the decline will continue until it meets support. This support is for the most part inside short covering both for profit and for stabilization of the market and is some of the long stock sold to the traders at higher prices.

This decline can stop anywhere under the Buying Day Low but from our column in the book we know the range of declines of past Violations and we know that they stop within the fractional limits and are occasionally very severe but knowing the range and by watching the activity at this point we generally get an indication of a coming rally.

We watch the market very closely for support buying and for the decline to slow down and stop for we, also, want to buy at this point and we do. At the turning point the stock makes a low, then rebounds in fractions or in points— this depends on the severity of the decline—if severe accompanied with activity, the churning up and down will be in a wider range of prices than if the decline was quieter and more normal, however, you will notice a considerable amount of trading at this point for a brief period, then the activity slows down and the market becomes comparatively quiet, the market goes dead but with the prices up a little from the extreme low reached on the decline. The quiet market may just penetrate the Buy Day Low fractionally and then trade a fraction above this low until a rally starts or the market starts to recover.

We buy on the above described action and at the market and expect the rally to start from this point, however, a support point here may only be temporary and another small decline may take place after a fractional rally that would establish a new low by a point or so but had the Violation been fairly deep, plus the points decline in the 'D' column—the spread from the Short Sale High to Buy Day Low—the over-all decline could be considerable and the chances are the rally would start from either of these low points and after all this probably would be the third session of a decline and 'remember' we are not buying on the top of a three days rise, either, as many traders do.

In the case where these two lows are made and had we bought at or near the first low, another small decline should not upset us, even though, it was against us for a point or so, for after the rally started and the probabilities would favor a rally from this last low our loss on paper would generally be only temporary and would be quickly made up.

After the rally starts it will generally make up all the Violation decline and this, then, would bring the price up to the Buying Day Low Point, now right at or through this point is our sure profit Selling Objective or at least a chance to get off the 'hook' in case you had made a 'too soon' purchase. From this Buy Day Low or a little above it, the decline may start in again.

From this point—the Buy Day Low—if the rally continues, it begins to 'wipe out' what we call the Real Decline and this is the units points shown in the 'D' column.

Each eighth above the Violation recovery, recovers a certain percent of the Real Decline, the more the rally is extended the more of this Real Decline is recovered and the rally may 'wipe out' all of this decline and continue higher. Many times when the 'D' column unit is small the R' column unit is large. Should the rally be so strong after it goes through the Buying Day Low and many times the activity picks up at this point and the trading is fast with the price reaching up to the top of the day and sometimes for a new high and then a slight 'dip'—then a rally just before the close. Should this kind of action take place after the penetration of the Buying Day Low, we would then begin to anticipate the possibilities of the penetration of the Primary Selling Objective—The Buy Day High—and we would not hesitate a minute before selling out on this penetration before the close.

Remember we are buying on a Selling Day and we must sell out before the close of the market and a reasonable level at which to sell our Long stock, assuming the Violation decline has been recovered, would be to sell when one third to two thirds of the amount of the decline in the 'D' column had been recovered.

We don't follow this rally, too far, and are not trading for the last eighth but for a profit and position for our next play and the next play would favor a decline and the next day is a Short Sale Day.

We watch this full rally, even though, we have sold out lower down—or just after the price went through the Buy Day Low on the rally—for the amount of reaction before the close or it may close right on the top price for the day, however, in any event a strong close would indicate a further rally, with an Up opening for a high made FIRST on Short Sale Day, yet, after a rally that would recover a two or three days decline, in one session may open off. This should not surprise you, you must expect it.

The rally from a Buying Day Low Violation made FIRST is caused by short covering and the start of the movement is usually engineered from the inside, the large short interest seems to be that part of the covering movement that carries the price up to and through the LOW of Buying Day and exhausts itself around this point. The extended and over-extended short interest and those traders that sold short, too near the bottom noting the strength of the rally after it gets started, are forced to cover and their buying is usually done in haste, therefore, the rally is fast, active and the spread between transaction is wide and this action many times causes the price to reach up to and through the HIGH of Buying Day. The extent and activity depends upon the size and urgency of the outside short interest.

The 'take off' from a period of accumulation, also, starts with a 'run in' of the shorts but usually 'they' try to conserve some part of it—for a good size short interest is potential strength at any stage of the move—generally, in the above case, it appears at times that the intent is to make all the shorts cover in the same session.

Buying on a Buying Day Low Violation made FIRST is for the most part buying against this short interest—inside and outside—but you are generally in good company when buying at this point in an Uptrend Trading Area. A rally caused by short covering is weak and that is why we don't follow it too far.

When the demand caused by this short covering is filled the stock then generally 'sells off' until it again meets with inside support.

Most of the Violations are found in the Downtrend Trading Areas, they must of a necessity make lower bottoms and the Downtrend is usually a session or two longer.

We watch the spread from the Buying Day Low to the Low of Violation and note if this spread is wide enough to make profit—that is, if we bought on the extreme low of Violation and sold out at or through the Low of Buying Day, should the stock rally back this high. When the decline is severe at this point the rally may not carry back as high as the Low of Buying Day, the rally would be 'dull' and the market quiet and would show the lack of buying by going 'dead' on the top, then the decline would perhaps start in again from this point. This kind of action would be an indication of a downtrend of more than the day to day kind, so in buying on this wide spread reaction, we would have to take whatever profits we could get, on whatever rally took place and the place to take them would be just as the rally began to hesitate and stopped. Should the spread be narrowed, more normal that is fractionally or a point or so, it would show the price holding, with covering and support buying, so we could expect more from any rally from this point.

A big decline takes times to consolidate around the low point, usually one or two session, before a good recovery rally sets in, therefore, the 'R' Rally Column Units are usually small after a large 'D' Column decline, unless the technical position of the market is strong enough to make the shorts cover in a hurry.

As a rule we don't expect too much of the immediate rally following a severe decline but when the market starts to recover and with activity it at times regains a large part—sometimes all the 'D' column loss and at times it sells through for a penetration of the Buying Day High.

The main import we are concerned with here, is to get off the 'hook' without a loss or as little as possible, for having bought near the low on a Buying Day and then to be caught in a Violation by reason of a down opening on a Selling Day, we have a loss, at least temporary but usually after a two or three days decline the Violation will be recovered and with a certain percent of the 'D' Column Unit.

We always sell on a recovery that makes up the Violation—of the Buying Day Low—and try to get some part of the rally above this point but we do not hold on too long, and hope for more rally and we don't let it bother us should the price go higher after we sell out. With reference to the below Plate—the rally after going through the 226 1/2—the Buy Day Low—may show signs of exhausting itself and right at or through this point the stock may start to decline again. We don't follow the rally, too far, for this reason...

The trading for the three days would have been as follows:

- Sell short on the penetration of 234 1/2
- Decline is severe for one session—above the average in points.
- Cover short—same session—on dullness around any low.
- (see Short Sale Day Chapter)
- (wide decline in same session)
- Wait for Buying Day to go 'long'.
- Buy on penetration of 228 1/2 when decline slows down or stops.
- Buy Low made FIRST—closing price up from low of the day—expect up-opening.
- Down opening—most of gain lost—sell on next rally.
- Violation low made FIRST—expect rally.

- Sell 'long stock' at or through the Buy Day Low of 226 1/2.

In the March Soybeans Future—SH—assuming a purchase at 227—on Buying Day—this is one half cent above the low, the decline is large and above the average for a 'D' column decline, with the Buying Day Objective (2) points under the previous low—the Short Sale Day Low—this point is, also, within our average for buying.

The stock closed up—on Buying Day—and we expected a higher opening on Selling Day, we did not get it. The stock opened down and declined quickly to 225 1/4 or (1 1/4) points Violation and at this point we would have had a loss of (1 3/4) points on paper. The Buy Day Low Violation was made first and the Violation was the third day of a decline, we expected the stock to rally and it did.

The rally quickly recovered the Violation decline and we are immediately alert for a place at which to sell out our long stock and this is somewhere at or through or above the Buy Day Low of 226 1/2.

After the Violation loss has been recovered, we keep a record of each transaction above this price—The Buy Day Low—we enter on our Work Sheet, on a pad with pencil or in our minds, these recovery prices as they appear on the 'tape' as the stock rallies.

We note the first price on the 'tape' at 227 or (1/ 2) pt., the first recovery 'tick' thru the 226 1/2—the Buy Day Low—and any recovery above this price is figured as a certain percent recovery of the decline in the 'D' column.

Many times a stock in a movement of this kind, at this point, will j-u-s-t come up to it or slightly exceed it, so we must sell out at or after it has been penetrated.

Should the action at this point be slow, it may just about reach or penetrate it but should the activity increase through and above this point the rally may carry through for a much deeper penetration, it can and does, at times, even rally far enough to penetrate the Buying Day High. See (SH) Plate—January Friday 21st.

At times, the recovery makes up all the 'D'

column unit loss and more.

We watch the transaction on the tape and we sell at the market at any point—at through and above the 226 1/2—the market at a point like at this will generally prepare you or give you a 'tip' on the coming action by slowing down, hesitating or stopping before a reversal or the activity will increase and the rally will continue on up but in many cases, just through this point will be the top for the rally from a Buying Day Low Violation. In the case of (SH) the rally stopped above this point—at 229—and then declined to 227 3/4, at the close of the market.

The column of figures at the Left Side of Work Sheet are the 'ticks' as they appeared in order on the tape until the top was reached at 229 and at this price the recovery of the (9) point decline of the 'D' column was approximately 27.7% or slightly below a one third recover—usually considered a minimum—not counting the (1 1/4) Points Violation recovery.

The above paragraphs point out more of an 'exit' from a bad situation and shows that a trader need not take big losses, if indeed a loss would have been taken in this case but so long as these situations exist in speculation a trader must know how to protect his capital.

This situation—only in reverse—happens about (50%) of the time where a trader can make his initial purchase on a Buying Day Low where no Violation occurs. The Violations occur about (35%) of the time, on an average, taking the total trading swings during the life of a grain future or a stock, during [its] ordinary up and down move with the general market.

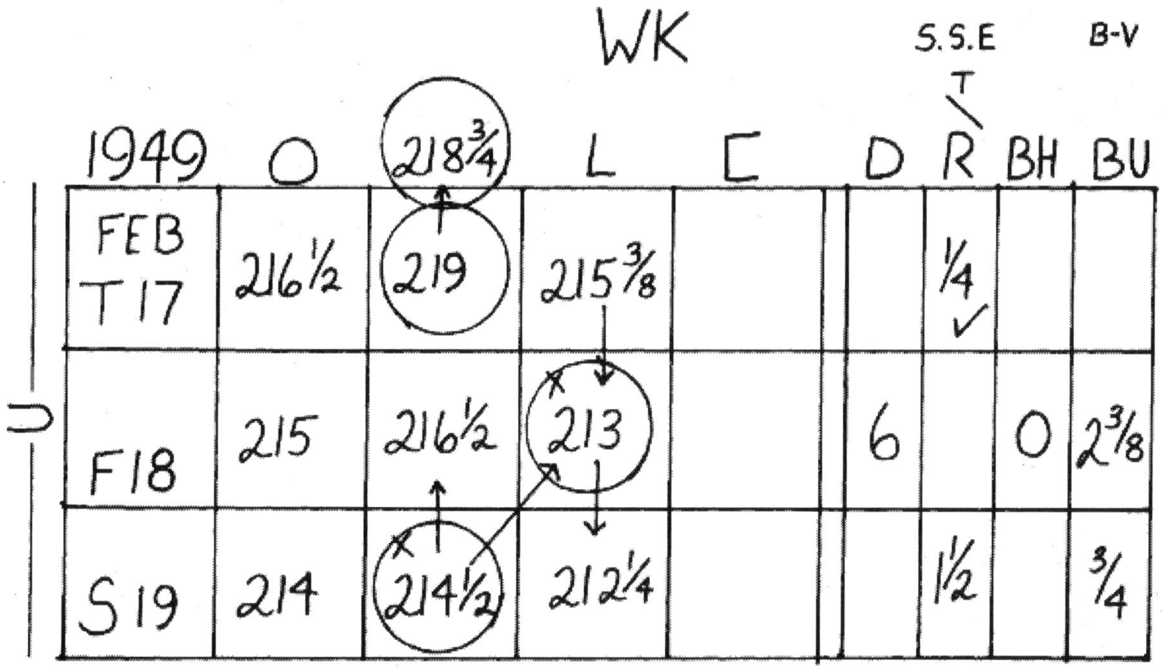

WK   S.S.E   B-V

1949	O	218¾	L	E		D	R	BH	BU
FEB T17	216½	219	215⅜				¼ ✓		
F18	215	216½	213			6		0	2⅜
S19	214	214½	212¼				1½		¾

FIGURE 4

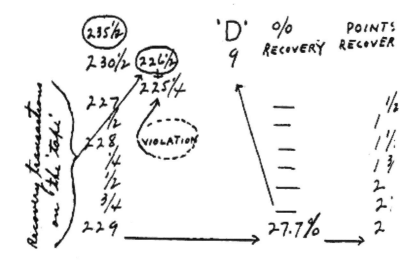

SH WORK SHEET

FIGURE 4

CHAPTER 7
A SELLING DAY

When the low is made FIRST on a Buying Day and the closing price is up from the low and nearer the high of the day, we look for and expect an up-opening and a penetration of the Buying Day High to sell on—on the Selling Day—and these penetrations occur more often in an Up-trend Trading Area.

On a Selling Day, should you sell out, too soon, after a penetration you lose some of your probable profits, so that in an Up-trend Area, you must expect not only slight penetrations but 'deeper ones' for the tops must be broken on the upside and be progressively higher.

The activity of the market after penetrations is a good sign to watch, also, after small 'D' column decline units.

From a strong closing on a Buying Day when the opening—of Selling Day—is up and wide—and this will generally be a penetration of the Buying Day High—We sell out 'at the market', without waiting for the next transaction to appear on the tape after the opening price. The price may go higher after we sell out and many times it does—so what—the opening price may be the high and is many times and a reaction may start from the next transaction after the opening price that could take the stock down much lower. We sell and 'at the market' and are not concerned with how high the price may go after we sell out.

When a purchase is made on a Buying Day Low and shows a good gain above this low—at the close—then should this gain be partly lost on the opening of—Selling Day—or opens at the Buying Day closing price—Sell out, 'at the market' without waiting for the next transaction to appear on the tape. Should the opening on—Selling Day—be down and decline further from the opening price—Sell out on any rally from the low of this decline and this point would be—at, through and above the low of Buying Day—should the rally carry back this far—this is now your Primary Selling Objective, instead of the Buying Day High.

On a stalled opening or where the opening and previous close are the same, the trader sells 'at the market' immediately upon seeing the opening price—should the following prices after the opening be up, his order is in and will be executed on a rising trend and he gets just that much more of the rally—should the following prices be down, his loss will be much smaller—his order is in—in time to 'duck' the real 'sell off' and he is out of the market quick and probably at the very inception of a declining trend. The price he gets for his stock will probably be slightly above or below what he paid for it on the previous day—the Buying Day.

Many traders at this point do nothing—if the stock starts up after the opening they wait to see what will happen—if the stock starts down after the opening price they wait for a rally to 'get out'—most likely the expected doesn't happen, either way and the net result is a greater loss.

For a reaction to take place from so short a rally—the low of Buying Day—indicates a weak up-trend and will generally 'fall short' of a penetration of the Buying Day High—the Selling Objective—even though the decline does not violate the Buying Day Low—Sellout, just the same, should the opening be down from the Buying Day Close. The stock does rally at times but we should not get this 'dip' so soon—the stock or future should have opened up and continued the rally further—if the immediate trend is higher.

It is the better 'play' to take a small loss at this point—should it be a loss, than to hold on a chance a much greater reaction.

Had you bought your 'long' stock somewhere near the Buying Day Low, you will probably get out with a small profit or an even break.

A Buying Day purchase must show a profit—that is, the spread from the low to the closing price and not lose it on the opening of—Selling Day—The above action does not favor your play so get out as cheap as you can.

Your Selling Objective, would be, at or through the High of Buying Day on a Selling Day but when this decline occurs with or without a Buying Day Low Violation, instead of a continuation of the rally—we change the Selling Objective and now make it—at or through the Low of Buying Day.

Should the decline stop within a fraction or a point or so and should the rally start with the activity picking up as the price sells through the Low of Buying Day and shows no hesitancy just above this Low, the rally may carry further—even penetrate the High of Buying Day—and it does, at times. We would then switch back to our Primary Selling Objective, that of selling—at or through the Buying Day High. We would sell out on this penetration before the close.

The Yearly Tables, show approximately (66) penetrations on—CK May Com—and (55) penetrations on WK May Wheat—out of a total of (100) Selling Objectives. See (SH) Plate for failures to penetrate and selling through Buying Day Low points, also, selling stock bought on Buying Day Low Violations.

Knowing how to trade on these kinds of plays are our only concern, for they are the trouble 'spots' and we have no way to anticipate their happening—except news that is announced after the market closing.

The more regular action of strong closings on Buying Days—with up-openings and penetrations of Selling Day Objectives are clear sailing and take care of themselves.

In this case—WK—made the high FIRST at 214 1/2 but part of the gain at close of Buying Day was lost on the opening of Selling Day. We sell our long stock on any rally following a decline at a point like this—at, through and above the Low of Buying Day. The stock if going higher should have opened up and continued the rally but we are not concerned with what it should do, we try to act on what it actually does—we follow the market and never try to make it.

The stock opened at 214 and rallied (1/2) point above the opening and our 'play' is to sell on any rally from a decline or down opening on a Selling Day—and 'at the market'.

After this (1/2) point rally the stock began to sell down and made the Buying Day Low Violation LAST and closed almost 'flat'.

Had your purchase been made near the Buying Day Low, your loss would not have been very much, even had you paid (214) for it but in holding on and hoping for more rally it could have been much more.

The recovery of the 'D' column unit decline of (6) points was (1 1/2) points—shown in 'R' column or 25%—the recovery rally.

In the case of—SH—it opened at 227 but declined FIRST and rallied LAST but with—WK—it rallied FIRST and declined LAST. See (SH) Plate Saturday 19th.

This is the reason why the signals have got to be watched carefully and these signal[s] mark[ed] 'X' FIRST and 'Y' LAST make the difference between being right or wrong on the trend.

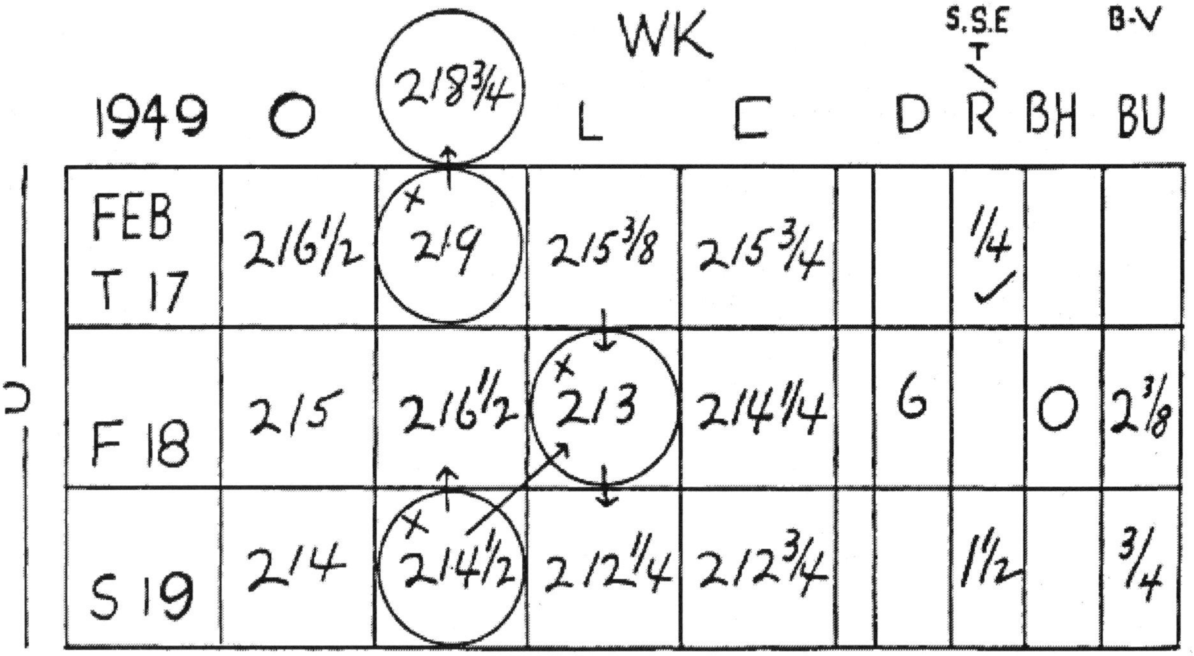

WK

1949	O	218¾	L	E		D	S.S.E T R	BH	B-V BU
FEB T 17	216½	x 219	215⅜	215¾			¼ ✓		
F 18	215	216½	x 213	214¼		G		O	2⅜
S 19	214	x 214½	212¼	212¾			1½		¾

FIGURE 5

38

CHAPTER 8
A SHORT SALE DAY

Let us assume the close on a Selling Day was strong, which in turn would indicate an up-opening and a continuation of the up-trend, the stock or future opens up and penetrates the Short Sale Objective—the Selling Day High—after the penetration we watch for a slowing down of the move, we are watching to detect if the price is meeting with resistance, if the selling at this point is overcoming the buying.

The selling we are looking for at this point is inside short selling and it gradually overcomes the unwise long buying by the traders at the top of this rally—or it stops the rally abruptly and the decline starts right in many times from the opening prices.

Many times at the top of a Short Sale Day, one or two futures or stocks will be made to appear strong by 'putting' them up a little higher while the others seem to resist further buying. You will notice when 'they' are rallying one future or stock that all the others will just 'hold or sell off' a little—this is done to create an air of strength and to test the buying power of the public and to put out short sales in all the others under the cover of strength in the ones they are 'putting' higher.

When it is clear that there is no further buying power the reaction starts—under the weight of these sales and short sales. The intent of 'those' making the market not to put the price higher makes the stock—the best kind of a short sale.

This same action takes place on a Buying Day, only in reverse, all futures and with stocks—will make low prices—then one or two are 'put down' for a new low while all the others hold—when there is no more selling coming into the market, the rally starts, including those that were used to influence the market.

We make our Short Sale—at through and above the High of Selling Day—on a Short Sale Day.

Had the high of Short Day been reached after a rally from the last Buying Day Low Point a reaction would probably be in order, since it would be the (3rd) day up.

We try to make all short sales on the high made FIRST on penetrations of—Selling Day Highs—'This is the most favorable action for your play'—we would not 'put out' a short sale where the stock or future opened down and declined future, without a rally, for this action would carry the implications that rally, should it start later in the session, may cause the closing price to be up near the high of the day and this would be making the high LAST on a Short Sale Day, indicating a 46 future rally, and an up-opening but where the stock opened at the same price as the previous close and declined early in the session and then rallied higher than the opening price or for a penetration of the Selling Day High—we would 'put out' a short sale just as this rally began to exhaust itself after the penetration. This action is not as favorable to our trade as the above.

When a reaction takes place after a penetration of the Selling Day High and the movement is in 'no hurry' and the stock just trades down, we stay short anticipating our covering point, next day, on the Buying Day. We can cover the short sale when we buy our 'long' stock or perhaps a little before—to trade in this way gives you a little more time to concentrate on your Buying Day Objective—this point for both covering your short and your purchase will be—at a little above or below the low of previous day—the Low of Short Sale Day.

Should the 'sell off' be severe and with activity—during the Short Sale Day session we cover our short sale on dullness, near the low of this reaction or if and when we have a profit. We are then out of the market and we stay but, we don't buy any long stock on the reaction. We wait for our next play which is that Buying Day Objective, no matter what the market does after we 'cover' and get out.

The stock or future can in this case rally fast—from the severe decline—and close strong and this would indicate that a high would be made FIRST on the next day—the Buying Day and would be another chance for a short sale, for a high made FIRST on a Buying Day, generally has some kind of a 'sell off'.

By taking our profits on this fast decline it strengthens our position, in case, the decline from this rally does not go as low on the next day, our Buying Day and we may have to buy at a Higher Bottom.

By this is meant that any profits made on the short sale can be used to reduce the cost of Buying a Higher Bottom—this is averaging but it is carried out in two separate trades.

Should you sell short, too soon, after penetration and it happens to be one of those occasional times when the price goes through for a more than average penetration, the trade will be against you, temporarily, however, a rally so active and strong that would cause a penetration of this kind would no doubt meet with profit taking and higher up short selling, both inside and professional which would cause the stock or future to react or decline low enough for you to 'cover' with a small loss, profit, or even break before the close.

These more than average penetrations are usually the fast rallies back following a severe decline and widen the trading swings both up and down for a few sessions, then the movement slows down and continues [its] trend, up or down, depending on which way is to be the future movement.

After a sharp decline followed by a rally the stock usually declines again to the low point reached on the first decline and it may hold above this point or go lower. This is the reason after covering our Short Sale—on the Short Sale Day—why we let the 'long side' of the market alone and wait for the second decline which generally occurs on the Buying Day.

This second decline may 'fall short' of reaching the low point made on the first decline, we then buy at this Higher Bottom and it is generally profitable—for if the stock is being supported and is not going lower, it will go higher—and generally where the stocks hold a Higher Bottom on a Buying Day, the price rallies high enough to make a profit.

When a Short Sale is made on a Short Sale Day—even on a penetration—of the Selling Day High—then declines from this high but at the low point of this decline the market becomes quiet and dull (with perhaps a few transactions at the same low price) then begins to rally—Cover your short sale, and just as the rally starts, the indication then, is for a strong close and the stock may even make a new high for the day. Had the short sale been 'put out' through and above the penetration, it can be 'covered' with little loss and perhaps with a small profit. The trade does not favor your play, so buy back your stock and stay out of the market. To continue to hold on could eventually cause a big loss. The rally starting from this low that would make up all the decline and a new high would be a quick 'run in' of the shorts and while holding the top price at the close, could be the end of the rally, with a down opening the next day, however, the rally is an indication of a further up-trend and a higher opening, but with no way to anticipate this move, better trade is to cover and stay out. A higher opening and a further advance would be a high made FIRST on a Buying Day, with the probabilities of a joint at which the short sale could be 'put out' again—or just wait and watch for a 'sell off' of a buying 'spot' to go 'long'.

A trader begins to anticipate a short sale after the close of a Selling Day session—First note the closing price and [its] relation to the high and low of the day—and if the close is up from the low and nearer the high or if the close is down from the high and nearer the low. The high closing indicates an up-opening and these up-opening generally occur in the Up-trend Areas, except, where the trend is being reversed from up to down. The low closing indicates a down-opening on the Short Sale Day, in the down-trend Areas, and where the trend is beginning to change from down to up. Next note if there was a Violation of buying Day Low—that is, if the low is under the previous low, if so, the rally starting from the low of Selling Day may not carry high enough on the—Short Sale Day—to penetrate the Selling Day High, it may come up near it by—first opening down and declining further, then rally later in the session for a strong closing—then many times the high of the rally—from Selling Day Low—is made FIRST on the next Buying Day, when preceded by the Violation and this is generally the (3rd) day of the rally and in a position for some sort of a decline. There will always be reversals at the openings—at times—from what we expect, due to news given out between sessions, however, it is seldom important enough to cause a reversal of the trend, after it has been established—after a trend has been running for some time with the price up or down, then a down-opening from a strong close or an up-opening from a weak close may be the beginning of the change of trend either way.

An up-closing on the Selling Day—in the Up Trend Area—indicates an up-opening on the—Short Sale Day—and this action is the rally that may cause the penetration of the—Selling Day High and FIRST and is the rally we use for our short sale—we 'put out' the 'short' at and through this penetration—generally the stock or future will react from this high made FIRST—but in the case where this Violation of Buying Day occurs, the stock many times rallies, from this decline and closes up, making the high LAST indicating a further up-trend, and a high made FIRST on the Buying Day.

This action explains the reason—when we 'put out' a short sale, even when there is no penetration—we 'cover' the short sale near the low of this decline, should the stock or future show any rallying tendencies—and the first signs would be a decrease in the activity near the low, with a hesitating action, quiet and dullness for a short period—then the activity picks up and each several transactions begins to hold a little of each gain.

This is a different movement from the rally that starts from the Low on a Buying Day—without this Violation—and proceeds in the more normal way, to a high on a Short Sale Day. See (RZ) Plate—October 13, 14, 15th.

The 'D' column units compared with the 'R' column units show the trend continuing up or down, reversing itself or forming a trade range.

Check back over the 'D' column units and note the spreads of the recent past several weeks and note if the spreads have been running wide enough to make a profit had you sold 'short'—if not, wait until the movement begins to widen.

The square at Left side of the Weekly Column gives the total of the fluctuating declines.

When a stock or future opens down on a Short Sale Day and declines further—let it alone—for not knowing what it might do, it does not favor your play. In your daily trading you will find plenty of Selling 'spots' made on penetrations and FIRST that are more favorable.

In 'putting out' a short sale on a penetration made FIRST it will generally be after a rally of two or three days and in most cases we are not selling at bottom prices or at lows of reactions because the stock or future looks so weak at these times.

Check the Yearly Plates and study the action that precedes and follows the penetrations and failures to penetrate Selling Day Highs, on Short Sale Days. See (SH) Plate for Short Sale Days when preceded by Buying Day Low Violations.

CHAPTER 9
A SHORT SALE AT HIGH OF BUYING DAY MADE FIRST

A Short Sale 'put out' at the high of Buying Day made FIRST on the penetration of the Short Sale Day High, should be covered on the reaction, whenever it sells down enough for a profit or on the first indications of dullness around the reaction low, for short selling on the Buying Day High made FIRST generally is a weak short sale—when prices are relatively low—especially in an Uptrend Trading Area—for the decline is of short duration when the trend is just starting up from the low point of the last Downtrend Area.

A Short Sale made on the high of Buying Day when it is made FIRST should always be covered during the Buying Day session, no matter how much lower the stock might look and because you should not short of a stock, at a point, where, in most cases, it is wiser to be long and generally it is the better trade to be long on a Buying Day, in an Uptrend Area.

In this case the stock or commodity future opens up and goes a little higher, it may or may not penetrate the High of Short Sale Day, then generally it reacts and around this reaction low we 'cover' should the market become quiet and dull. We then watch the market but need not be in too great a hurry to buy or go 'long' since, so far, the low is being made LAST on a Buying Day, with the possibilities that the stock may trade down lower with the indications of a 'flat' closing, in which case WE DO NOT BUY AT ALL, even though this low is under the previous low—the Low of Short Sale Day—which would ordinarily be our Buying Objective.

In this latter case of the low being made LAST we are anticipating a buying point on a Buying Day Low Violation—made FIRST—next day, when prices get within the range for Violations as shown in Violation Column in our book.

We cover a short sale quick on a Buying Day, when the stock acts 'tight' and resists an 'easy sell off' and we look ahead for a point on this day to go 'long' of the stock.

Never sell a stock or future short on a Buying Day, when it makes the low FIRST—by opening down—even though it is the third or fourth day of the rally. There is not enough spread and you can not make a profit with a reasonable certainty.

Don't let it bother you because you covered your short sale and after that the price went lower and is closing on the low for the day you have a profit and that is what you are trading for—quick small profits—Now, begin to look forward for a chance to buy a Buying Day Low Violation, next day, and this would generally be a strong buying point for the Violation would usually be made FIRST and early in the session and generally the rally from this low is profitable.

Usually in a strong Uptrend the stock will make the High FIRST on a Buying Day—about 35% of the time on an average—it then declines, then rallies and holds the gains for a strong closing. A trader sees the up-opening and a penetration or failure to penetrate the Short Sale Day High and notes the activity at or through this point, just as it slackens and stops, he sends in his order to sell—he then watches whatever reaction that takes place from this high and the activity around the low—if the stock shows no indication to rally but he waits before going 'long'. From this decline low the stock often rallies—in an Uptrend—and should it make a new top after this decline, by going higher than the opening price or the high of the first rally, he buys on any set back from this high, before the close of the market. He covers the short sale earlier as insurance, because he must anticipate just such a rally as might occur here.

In buying at this higher price on the set back before the close, he is not 'chasing' the price up, for he has a short sale profit to average the cost down, although each is considered an independent trade. This action indicates a strong close on the Buying Day and a strong Selling Objective, for this 'long' stock, next day.

We watch the spread between the Buying Day High and the price we paid for our 'long' stock and since we bought above the low of the day—we don't expect too much, since we are only trading for some part of this move and we must be ready to sell out in case of a higher opening on Selling Day or on the penetration of the Buy Day High.

The beginning of Downtrends, many times, start from a Buy Day High made FIRST and particularly so when prices are comparatively high. The high is made FIRST (a high made FIRST on any day is usually an up-opening from the previous close and this may establish it or the price may rally further, after the opening) then the decline starts but so long as the rallies from any low point 'fall short' the high has been registered for the session—this may sound silly but carefully watch the days when this action takes place—you will observe many attempts to rally the stock and some of them will appear pretty strong but with the few exceptions, the high prices made early usually stand.

With the above after the decline starts, the activity is on the down side—the stock makes faint attempts to rally but doesn't seem to get very far—the activity dries up at the top of these rallies and the market becomes dull and quiet, then the decline starts in again from these lower tops. On an action of this kind we don't even think about the 'long side' of the market, even though it is a Buying Day. Had we gone short higher up, we watch the market but we 'cover' our short sale before the close.

A weak closing on a Short Sale Day, may indicate a lower opening on the Buying Day—and we get set to buy on the low made FIRST—yet, the opening may be up, on account of some news announcement between the sessions causing the high to be made FIRST—on Buying Day—perhaps a little short covering—then a decline may start from this high—a short sale made at this top is covered on this first decline with a smaller profit, for from this low or lower a

short covering move could start that would carry the price up for a new high and end the session with a strong close, this rally would then cause the high to be made LAST—in this case the 'insiders' might think the news was worth a little further discounting than at the opening or higher prices—having covered—we watch the prices around this extreme low for a few transactions at about the same price and if, at this low, prices were under the Low of Short Sate Day or holding a Higher Bottom—if the latter, so much the better, it shows higher support—we buy on this 'quiet spot'—any fast active rally that might take place from this low would be short covering started from the 'inside' and a strong rally from here up to the close would generally be a weak rally, so, sellout before the close to protect your profits, for there is always the possibility that prices may be down at the opening, next day, the Selling Day. Had you bought and this rally did not take place—sell out before the close, for the indications would be for lower prices—the low was made LAST on a Buying Day.

A high made FIRST may be established by opening down on a Buying Day but would be of no interest to us for short selling—this would be causing the low to be made LAST—the probabilities would favor a rally from this low before the close, for in this case the stock would be selling off from a previous high price—our Buying Day Objective is based on a decline of one or two days, from higher prices. Any rally from this low that would make a new top, after this decline, would reverse the high made FIRST—it would then be made LAST—and this then would cause the Buying Day Low to be made FIRST a strong confirming action for the 'long side' and generally the close would be strong, an indication for a strong Selling Objective, next day, for the 'long' stock.

Generally where you get a wide spread from low to close, after the stock has sold down from higher prices, you are getting your profit in the same session, so take it in the same session and don't enter the market again (in the same stock or future) until the Short Sale Day, no matter what the stock does in the interval.

The reason for short selling on the Buying

Day high made FIRST, is that had the rally been in progress from the last Buying Day Low, it would be the (4th) day up and the rally would be in the process of exhausting the upswing and in many cases the stock makes the high on the Buying Day—when preceded by a Buying Day Low Violation, it is being made after (3) days of rally.

CHAPTER 10
FAILURES TO PENETRATE

We will start with a stock or commodity future at or near the top of an Uptrend Trading Area, assume the uptrend had been under way for a week or two or more and the price gains were Five Cents or Points or more from the low reached on the previous Downward Trading Area. Now, should the top be in process of being reached the extreme high would generally be made on a relatively fast, active, wide move with volume—in the case of stocks—on the commodity 'tape' we have no volume, so we watch the comparative activity of the market. After the extreme high is established the price would probably break back under the high point and the trading for the remainder of the session and the closing price would generally be slightly under this top. This action is caused by 'inside' selling, by 'those' who think the price is high enough, at least temporary. Enough selling takes place to stop the rise but not enough to break the price wide open, however, at times, this does happen.

On a run up of this kind it attracts a following of 'outside long' buying and this demand is filled during the trading that takes place under this low and at the opening, the next morning. Many times the supply is more than the demand at the higher price and the stock opens down and declines further, however, a rally follows from this low but this rally is accomplished on a quieter market with decreased activity and volume in the stock—activity in the commodity—the rally fails to reach the extreme high, then the decline starts again from this failure.

When this is the top, the Uptrend Trading Area is now changing to a Downtrend Area and low points as they are made will be penetrated after rallies and the rallies will progressively fail to reach former highs.

At the bottom Trading Areas, when the trend is changing from Down to up, the stock or future makes a low on the same kind of market action, only in reverse, the extreme low is usually made on relatively heavy volume and activity, then the stock rallies from this low, with light or heavy volume but the decline takes place on greatly decreased volume and activity—the heavy buying at this low for support and other purposes is held, therefore, the pressure on this decline is not so great and the stock fails to go as low, or it may penetrate the first established low point fractionally.

Failures to penetrate the immediate previous highs and lows, do occur both up and down in an Up or Down Trading Area. These are usually arrested moves due at times to the news of the moment but in most cases we get a forecast of them by watching the closing prices—compared to the highs and lows of the day—weak or 'flat' closings forecast lower prices with the results that rallies from these declines many times fail to penetrate the Selling Objectives—on the Selling and Short Sale Days.

In the case of the Higher Buying Day Low point, the failure to penetrate on the down side—the Short Sale Day Low—the stock shows support and the chances of recovery of a good part and perhaps all of the 'D' Column Units, the stock is receiving only stabilizing support and can go lower, after a rally. Many times the close will be up from the low on a Buying Day but the opening price—on Selling Day—will be the same as the closing price, with a failure on any rally from here to penetrate the Selling Day Objective—the High of Buying Day—then the decline starts from this failure and the stock makes a Violation of the Buying Day Low LAST.

It is this kind of an opening on Selling Day—at the Buying Day closing price—that causes us to sell on any rally or even on the next transaction on the tape, after the opening and we use the Buying Day Low, as our Selling Objective.

The Violation of a Buying Day Low, in most

cases, forecasts the failure of the rally to penetrate the High of Buying Day—on the Selling Day—at times, rallies do come up to and through the Buy Day High, but in many cases the rally fails after reaching up to and through the Buy Day Low. It takes rally to recover all the 'D' Column Units and to then rally high enough to penetrate the High of Buying Day. The Violation is, in itself, generally a three days or more decline and it seems to require a session or two to build up a rally that will penetrate the tops of selling days—the Selling and Short Sale Day—then the high in most cases is made FIRST or LAST on the next Buying Day.

Perhaps the best forecast of a failure to penetrate on the Selling Day would be revealed by the 'D' Column, in the severity of the decline, as shown by the size of this unit.

On a Short Sale Day, we can see the range of the 'sell off' as it is taking place by watching the spread from the high to the low. This spread gives you part and sometimes all of the range in advance of the Buying Day. A rally from this low with a higher closing price, indicates a failure to go lower—on the Buying Day—and this is what causes Higher Buy Day Bottoms and the Zero in the (BU) Column points them out. You can visualize and anticipate this Zero, so long as the price holds above—the Low of Short Sale Day—and where this Zero appears, it generally forecasts nearby higher prices.

In the beginning it might be well to study these failures to penetrate and the results of them before buying or short selling but you have got to recognize this action and trade on it, for while it is a most difficult 'play', at the same time many of the most profitable moves take place from failures to penetrate at both tops and bottoms.

The failures to penetrate Buying or Selling Objectives are not exceptions to our method of trading, for a little study of the past movements of stocks and commodity futures will reveal that this action takes place approximately 40% of the time on an average, at either of these points, therefore, this movement is a very definite part of the method as a whole.

The failures to penetrate the tops are usually found in the Downtrend Areas and when the trend is changing at the top and in most cases are forecast by weak or 'flat' closings on the Buying, Selling and Short Sale Days. At the bottoms, rallies before the close that hold, forecast up-openings and failures to go lower.

When a stock makes a high FIRST on a Selling Day with a penetration of the Buying Day High, then reacts and is selling nearer the low of the day at the close, the indications are for a lower opening on the Short Sale Day. Should the lower opening occur, after the decline the stock or future will make an attempt to rally, in most cases, and this rally will penetrate the—High of Selling Day—if the immediate trend is higher, however, should the rally fail to reach this Objective and at the top of this rally the activity dies out and the trading narrows down to a few transactions at about the same price, then begins to 'sell off', we would 'put out' a short sale on this declining trend and J-U-S-T as it starts. This would be the better play when prices are comparatively high for near the bottom of an Uptrend Area, there may not be enough room in the spread to make a profit.

Should you sell on this rally and the stock react and near this decline low, the stock show signs of 'tightness' by going quiet and the trading sort of 'bumps around at the same price' without making new lows—cover your sale and take your loss or profit on the first indications of this kind of action. At times the open will be down—on a Short Sale Day—and will continue down without any rally and not give you a chance for a trade. Should this kind of action take place, there isn't a thing you can do that would favor your play, except let it alone. You can look through your books for a more favorable trading Objective. You would probably have a book on a stock or future that would be a Buying Objective on this same day, if so, this would be the Objective to trade on, for it, too, would generally be down and would be making the low FIRST on a Buying Day. Any rally from this low would generally be profitable.

When the price falls to make a Short Sale Objective—the penetration of a Selling Day High— by a relatively severe decline at the opening, it is better to pass up the session and not try to 'put out' a short sale on the rally, should a rally take place, from this decline—the trade does not favor your play and there is always the possibility that any rally from this decline may hold, thereby, causing the high to be made LAST, with the indications of the continuance of the uptrend.

The amount of rally from a Short Sale Day Low, plus a higher opening causes a Higher Bottom and a failure to sell lower on the Buying Day.

The failure to sell as low on the Buying Day, reduces the decline unit in the 'D' Column—this shows the rally starting from the low of Short Sale Day—while the Buying Day Low Under—Short Sale Day Low—increases this decline unit.

The reduction of the unit in the 'D' Column is caused by and means a rally and the failure to sell as low, forecasting a probable penetration of the Selling Day Objective—the Buying Day High—while the increase in the unit in the 'D' Column means a decline and penetration with a forecast of a probable failure to penetrate the Selling Day Objective. That is why in buying a Higher Bottom it is profitable most of the time, for you are buying just after the rally started—from the low of Short Sale Day—while buying a Buying Day Under—under Short Sale Day Low—you are trying to catch a probable temporary low, before the rally starts. On Violations of Buying Day Lows made FIRST, the rally from this low fails—not always but in most cases—to penetrate the Selling Day Objective—the Buying Day High—that is why we use the Buying Day Low as our Selling Objective.

In the case of the Higher Buying Day Low, the stock or future shows support causing a rally and a strong close on the Short Sale Day—the decline from this rally, next day, on the Buying Day, fails to sell down through the previous low—the Short Sale Day Low—this rally on the Short Sale Day, is an indication of a Higher Buy Day Bottom and the failure to penetrate this low—low of Short Sale Day— reduces the decline unit in the 'D' Column and the forecast is for a larger unit in the 'R' Column, two days in advance.

Weak closings forecast failures to penetrate 'top side' on the rallies after declines, while strong closings forecast failures to penetrate 'down side' on the declines after rallies.

CHAPTER 11
THE TREND LINE AND TRADING AREAS

The line running along side of the Date Column, we use for the trend line of the market and while we don't use [its] primary term possibilities for our method of trading, we do use [its] implications for Bull and Bear intermediate swings and we always keep the Seasonal Trends in mind.

This longer term line is broken up into the shorter swings and these are our Trading Areas and are moves of Five Cents or Points or more and there can be any number of these areas in the longer term or Seasonal Trends of the market.

We watch the highs and lows of these areas and the number of points move up or down and the time consumed in each move and particularly after a move of Two or Three Weeks in either direction.

In the Seasonal Trend Upward Swing we expect penetrations at—the tops of these Trading Areas and we watch for support and the progressive lifting of the bottoms after declines. We note the kind of Objective Day we are trading on, as the price nears or—is at the top of a previous area, since we can expect wider moves on the day of 'break thru' or penetrations. The same at the bottom of these areas in the Seasonal Downward swing.

One of the several kinds of our trading Objectives must end a move at the tops and bottoms, a Sale, Short Sale or a high made FIRST on a Buying Day, at the tops and a Buying Day Objective or a Violation of it, at the bottoms.

By concentrating all our attention on these smaller areas, we eliminate a lot of confusion, since there is no need to watch other than the highs and lows of the previous Trading Area.

When the High of the Area we are trading in, in the Up Seasonal Trend approaches the high of the previous Area, we look for a penetration of this top, when prices are comparatively low or failure to 'break thru' when prices are comparatively high. In other words we look for

supply at the tops and support at the bottoms or penetrations at either end with volume and activity.

We watch the kind of Trading Objective Day, when these penetrations are made for they generally are wide moves and at these points we can expect more and can hold on for deeper penetrations when prices are moving in our favor.

We watch for rallies to start from Buying Objectives and declines to start from Selling Objectives or from failures to penetrate at tops or bottoms.

Trading Areas vary in length of time and in number of points and there is no way of knowing in advance how long they will run, up or down, nor are we much concerned, however, the failure to penetrate the last high or low of a selling or buying Objective, especially after a move of two or three weeks, up or down, may be the changing of one trend to another.

We buy, sell and sell short in the Up and Down Trading Areas, generally, and in the Up Trends we can expect the Selling Objectives to be reached and penetrated and in the Down Trends we look for Buying Day Under moves—under Short Sale Day Low—and Buying Day Low Violations—this is the low under the Buying Day.

In the Down Trend Area, we can expect not only two decline sessions—the low of Short Sale Day and the Buying Day Low Under—to complete a move but we can expect Buying Day Low Violations before these rallies start.

In the Up Trend Areas, we can expect the corrective decline to be completed in one and perhaps the same session—this is the low made on a Short Sale Day, from a fast decline, with an active fast rally from this low up to the close—with the results that we get Higher Buy Day Bottoms and penetrated Selling Objectives, "This is the reason why we 'cover' a short sale when the decline is severe in the same session and equals the average of an ordinary decline that would require the time consumed in the movement from a High on Short Sale Day to the Low on a Buying Day".

We always keep in mind the immediate previous type of Trading Area—the Up Trend Area, made on wide daily rallies and declines are in most cases likely to maintain the same characteristics on the reaction or Downtrend. The fast and almost vertical Upward movements will generally show the same kind of action, only in reverse, the decline is severe and the drop precipitous with little or no spread on the daily rallies from the lows, until it nears the bottom of the decline.

On the fast Upward Movement compare the 'D' and 'R' Column Units—note the penetration mark over the 'R' Column Unit, also, the absence of the loss unit in the (3) day column—we do get toss swings in the Uptrend but generally the loss unit is fractional. Note: When the 'D' Column Unit is small the 'R' Column Unit is generally large.

On the fast Downward Movement the 'D' and 'R' Columns reverse themselves and the loss swing begins to show up in the (3) Day Column.

The very narrow 'line' Trading Area—see Chart on 'X' for 1944—is without movement enough to trade for a profit and nothing can be done about it, the market just doesn't have anything to give.

This period shows, perhaps the narrowest range a Leader Stock can reach and still show up daily, on the 'tape'.

The Industrial Average fluctuated in about a (16) point range during the entire year of 1944.

These 'patches' are but parts of these several kinds of trends—and are taken from both Bull and Bear Primary Markets, but are highly representative of the whole trend of which they are part.

We do find, regardless of the kind of trend—Up or Down—or the year in which they take place—the movements maintain the same daily trading characteristics.

Stocks do not have the same velocity of movement as grains and other commodities. They trade around highs and lows and spend more time in reaching a daily high or low, so that most of the time it is possible to buy and sell within an eighth or quarter of a point. A trader must not become so accustomed to the wider movements in commodities, as to expect the same movements in stocks.

While using U.S. Steel as an example—all other stocks exhibit the same pattern of movement and many others are better trading vehicles, their movement is wider and they have a broad daily trading range. It is not the intent to suggest any stock for trading purposes—the trader must select his own stocks and will be in a better position if he will make up a book on them and study it. Many stocks have 'set' habits and 'quirks' that a trader will learn to recognize after he gets acquainted with [its] movements. It is surprising, too, just how often a stock will move as expected.

By studying the Seasonal Trends on the charts, next pages, we can get a fairly reliable picture of the months of the year when grains, normally, sell at their highest and lowest prices. Stocks have no season.

The Trend Line should be alternated with different color inks, marking the Uptrend Line with Blue and the Downtrend Line with Red. This will separate them and you can get a complete picture of the whole area at a glance.

THE TREND LINE FOR THE DILETTANTE SPECULATOR

Those traders who can not attend the market sessions daily, can also trade at their convenience.

Suppose some other business came up as it does occasionally and it was not possible to come to the market place, well, this need not affect the trader, so far as keeping a line on the market and a trend for him to trade on, at the time he decides to reenter the market, even though, he has been absent for a week or a month.

Just so long as he kept his book in order he would always have a check on the market, so far as trading with this method is concerned.

It may be that he would find himself in some remote place and there were no papers or quotations available, he would not have to fill in the daily price entries, just so long as he kept the circles in his book in continuity.

Upon his return he would then only have to refer to the newspaper of the day before for prices and on the, day he decided to start trading he would know at once whether it would be wiser to buy or sell short, he could not use a Selling Day in this case for he would not have any 'long' stock to sell.

MARKET TRENDS

"Market" represents the correlation of opinions of buyers and sellers which results in sales. "Market" phases are used in market reports to indicate comparisons with conditions which prevailed on the previous day, or conditions expected on the day following, or both. Comparison of the present price level with past and future levels creates the "Market Tone".

Terminology - On market reports "market" phases are used in the following sense:

- MARKET STRONGER represents a condition of actual and general price advances.
- MARKET STRONG indicates an upward trend with a bullish market sentiment that anticipates further advances. May also be used to describe a situation where prices are at high levels and no immediate decline seems in prospect.
- MARKET FIRM indicates a condition of increasing confidence on the part of most sellers. Prices are either holding at the level of the day before or are a shade higher.
- MARKET STEADY represents a condition where there are no appreciable price changes or trends in either direction and no definite sentiment that any immediate market changes are in prospect.
- MARKET DULL represents a period of relative market inactivity but no definite tendency toward market changes.

- MARKET UNSETTLED indicates a condition of market uncertainty, with a lack of agreement on the part of the trade as to whether there is a stronger or weaker tendency to the market. It may also represent a waiting attitude pending the development or outcome of factors which might affect the, market such as storm damage, labor troubles, weather conditions, legislation, etc.
- MARKET WEAKER represents a condition of actual and general price declines.
- MARKET WEAK indicates a downward trend with a market sentiment that anticipates lower prices.
- MARKET DEMORALIZED is used only in unusual cases. It describes a condition wherein the market is oversupplied and sales cannot be made except at very low prices.

The above market phrases may be qualified as to degree by terms such as "slightly stronger", "slightly weaker", "about steady", "very dull", "quiet weak", "quiet firm", etc.

The trader who will commit these market phrases to memory will have a better understanding of the changing market sentiment and can use them to advantage in his buying and selling. Try to deduce from them what effect, if any, they could have on the next market session and on his present market position and for their forecast of the nearby market trends. The newspapers usually head-up their columns with these phases.

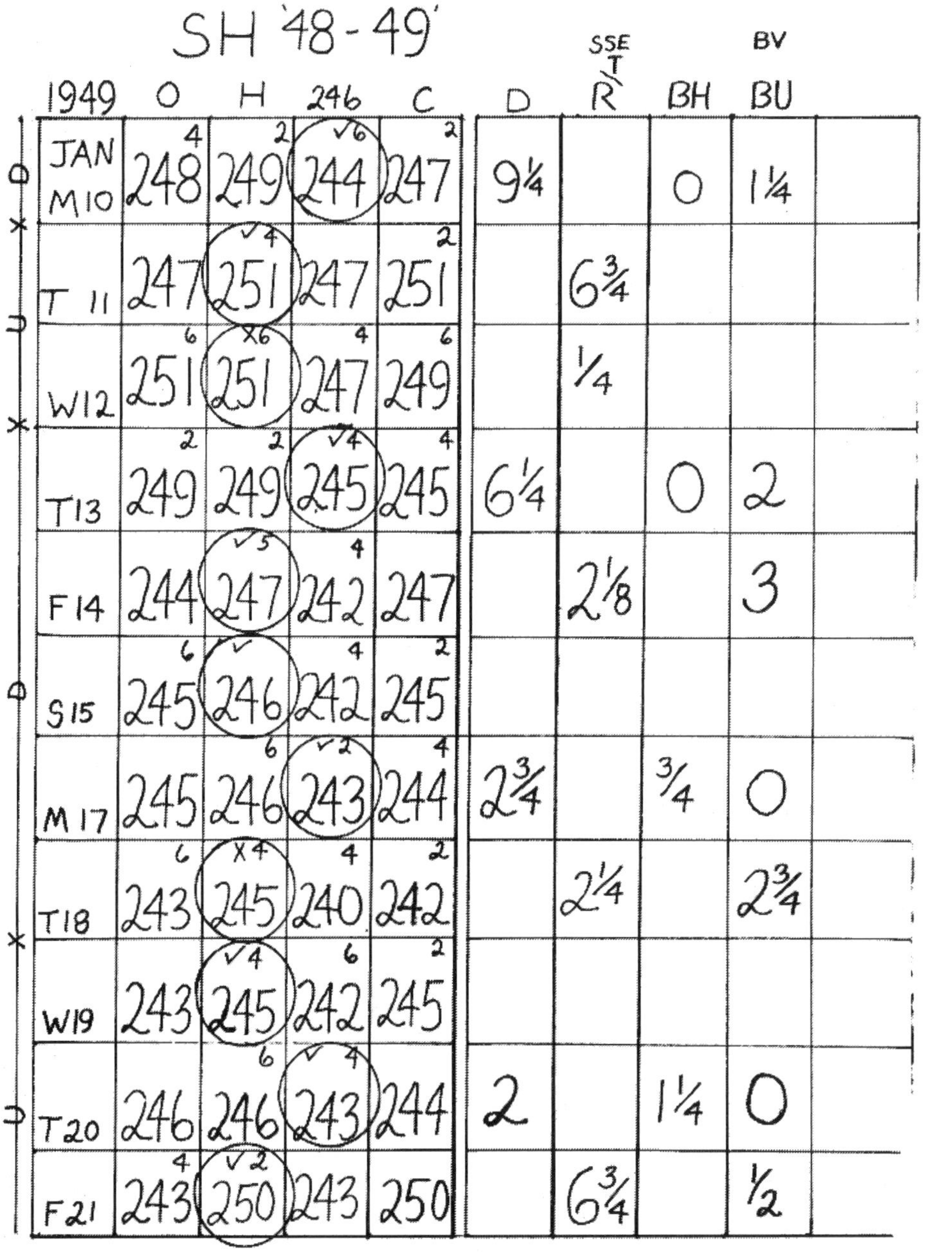

SH '48-49'

1949	O	H	246	C	D	R (SSE T)	BH	BU (BV)	
JAN M10	4 248	2 249	√6 244	2 247	9¼		0	1¼	
T 11	247	√4 251	247	2 251		6¾			
W12	6 251	X6 251	4 247	6 249		¼			
T13	2 249	2 249	√4 245	4 245	6¼		0	2	
F14	244	√5 247	4 242	247		2⅛		3	
S15	6 245	√ 246	4 242	2 245					
M 17	245	6 246	√2 243	4 244	2¾		¾	0	
T18	6 243	X4 245	4 240	2 242		2¼		2¾	
W19	243	√4 245	6 242	2 245					
T20	246	6 246	√ 4 243	244	2		1¼	0	
F21	4 243	√2 250	243	250		6¾		½	

FIGURE 6

• (A) Buy Day—market opened off—249 1/2 high made FIRST on sluggish rally—failed to penetrate Short Sale high—Sell Short—cover on decline on penetration of 246 Sat. 8th low—Buy Under is 1 1/4 points from S. Sale High—Buy around 244 3/4—market has time to rally—if no rally sell before close—rallied and closed strong—expect up opening and further rally tomorrow.

• (B) Opened at previous close to down 1/4—next immediate transactions are on the upside—watch the 249 1/4 as the selling Objective for your long stock—sell on the penetration thru and above—254 1/2 high being made LAST—close at high for the day—expect up-opening tomorrow for a short sale on penetration of today's high.

• (C) Opened up with a penetration of 254 1/2—high being made FIRST—sell short—this is the 3rd day up from Monday—market active and declining at 247 1/2 is off 4 1/2 points—fairly severe reaction—market trading around this low—cover short—decline can continue or can rally—being out, stay out—middle closing between high and low—tomorrow is a Buy Day—watch 247 1/2 at or below for a chance to buy—on an up-opening and further rally tomorrow try to get out a short sale.

• (D) Market opened down and declining—no chance for a short—good action for a buy low being made FIRST at 245 1/2 the Buy Under is 2 cents—this is about the average unit in the Buy Under Column—Buy at the market—don't expect a big rally following a big D Column unit decline—market not rallying looks like a flat closing—sell out before the close—expect down opening tomorrow with a chance to buy a Buy Day Low Violation made FIRST.

• (E) Opening down and declining—242 1/2 is now a 3 cents Violation being made FIRST—Buy at the market—sell out on any rally before the close—watch the 245 1/2 price—this is the selling Objective—at thru and above—this is the 3rd day down from 254 3/4—the strong closing and on high for the day is short covering and could be the end of the rally—on account of the Violation the price may fail to go as high tomorrow—Many times the High is made on the next Buying Day.

• (F) Market opened down—too much concession from previous close for a short sale—low is being made FIRST on a Short Sale Day—let it alone—market can rally before the close and make the high LAST—an uptrend indication—on account of Buy Day Violation at 242 1/2 yesterday we might get a high for a short sale made FIRST tomorrow—this would be the 3rd day up-market closed strong—expect further uptrend on Monday 17th.

• (G) Opened down 1/4 cent but market is rallying FIRST on Buy Day—Sell Short on the penetration of 246—cover sale at thru or above 242 1/2 or if and when you get a profit—watch 242 1/2 as your buying point—market is quiet and is trading at 243 1/4—the low is being made LAST but is holding a 3/4 cent Higher Bottom—buy around this price—market is closing up from the low—support is higher than yesterday—expect a further rally tomorrow.

• (H) Opened down at 243 3/4—Sell on any rally where Buy Day close gains are lost on Selling Day opening—the Selling Point to watch it at, thru and above the 243 1/4 the Buy Day Low—thru and above this point watch for the activity to dry up and the rally to stop—from this point and slightly above the decline can start again—Sell above this point if the market hesitates or stops—Violation at 240 1/ 2 made LAST of no use for trading—indicates weak Short Sale tomorrow—Expect high to be made on next Buy Day.

- (I) Opened up then sold down—no short sale the low is being made FIRST—stay out—the chances favor a rally later in the session with high made LAST—this day is like Sat. 15th on account of Violation of last Buy Day Low—the high is being made LAST—the closing is up—an up-opening tomorrow would be a penetration and a short sale above—also the 3rd day up from 240 1/2—on down opening the low would be in process of being made FIRST—watch for a Buying spot at, above or below 242 3/4—strong closing at high—indications for further uptrend.

- (J) Opened up with penetration of 245 1/2—sell short above the penetration—cover the sale on any decline around the 242 3/4 point the Short Sale Day low—wait for a chance to go 'long'—the market is not rallying and low is being made LAST but is holding a Higher Bottom—buy before the close—buying a Higher Bottom is usually profitable—expect a further rally tomorrow—today's action is the same as Mon. 17th.

- (K) Opened down made Violation FIRST at 243—market began to rally from here—this decline at opening catches us with 'long Stock' bought yesterday at close—on any rally from 243 we must watch for a place to sell out—the point is the Buy Day low 243 1/2—at or just above this point the activity slows down and the rally stops or it gains in momentum—the price having sold thru this point and with the activity picking up you now watch the 246 3/4 point, Buy Day High to be reached—sell at, or thru this point— Don't follow the rally further.

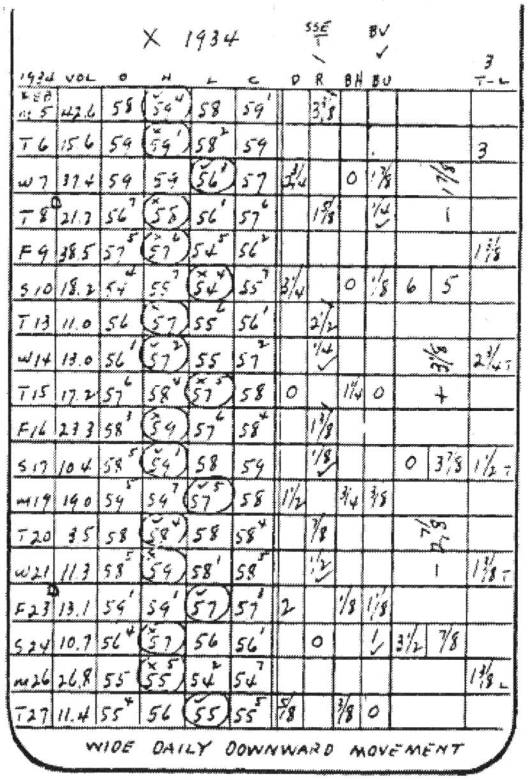

FIGURE 7

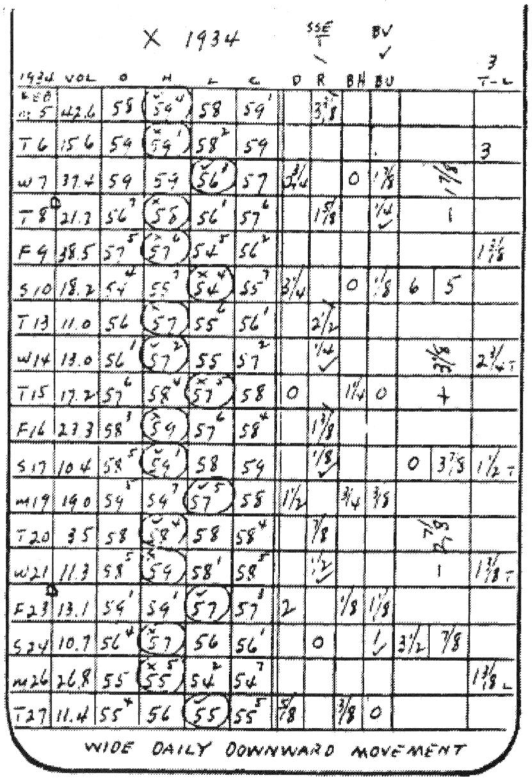

FIGURE 8

U.S. STEEL "X" — SSE T ╲ — BV ✓

1938	VOL.	O	H	L	C	D.	R	BH	BU.	±		3 T-L
MAR F11	17.5	50^{5}	51^{4}	50^{2}	50^{2}							5/8 L
S12	5.5	50^{2}	51^{2}	50^{2}	51	1/4		0	0	2	1 1/4	
M14	7.1	52^{4}	52^{6}	51^{6}	52^{4}		2 1/2					
T15	18.3	52^{3}	54^{2}	52^{2}	54^{2}		1 1/2					4 T
W16	31.2	53^{4}	53^{4}	50^{2}	50^{5}	4		0	2	0		
T17	9.0	51^{5}	52^{4}	51	51^{2}		3/4					
F18	27.0	51^{1}	51^{1}	48^{2}	49^{2}							7/8
S19	9.3	50^{7}	51^{3}	50^{5}	51	1/2		1/4	0	4 1/2	4 3/4	
M21	9.0	51^{7}	52^{2}	50^{5}	50^{7}		1 5/8					
T22	13.4	51	51^{4}	49^{2}	49^{5}							7/8
W23	25.8	49	49	47	48	4 1/2		0	2 1/4			
T24	18.0	48^{1}	49^{3}	47^{2}	48^{6}		2 3/8					
F25	36.4	47^{4}	48	44^{6}	44^{6}							1
S26	16.0	44^{3}	45^{6}	44	44^{3}	4		0	3/4	8 1/2	4	
M28	21.4	44^{2}	45^{2}	43^{5}	44^{1}		1 1/4		3/8			
T29	34.8	42^{3}	42^{3}	39^{5}	39^{6}							1 3/8 L
W30	27.4	39^{7}	41^{2}	39	39^{4}	3 3/8		0	5/8			
T31	23.2	40^{2}	41^{3}	38	39^{1}		2 3/8		1			

FAST DOWNWARD MOVEMENT

FIGURE 9

U.S. STEEL "X" — SSE T ╲ — BV ✓

1938	VOL.	O	H	L	C	D	R	BH	BU	±		3 T-L
JUN T21	24.5	45^{2}	46^{4}	45^{1}	46^{1}	1/4		1/8	0			
W22	35.2	45^{6}	48^{4}	45^{6}	48		3 3/8					
T23	50.7	48^{2}	51^{2}	47^{4}	50^{6}		2 1/4			+		6^{1} T
F24	44.3	51^{3}	53^{6}	51^{3}	52^{4}	0		2 1/2	0			
S25	27.4	51^{4}	54^{7}	51^{4}	54^{2}		3 1/2			1/4	6 7/8	
M27	33.8	53^{7}	54^{5}	52^{6}	53							3^{2}
T28	26.9	52^{4}	54^{3}	52^{4}	53^{1}	2 1/8		0	1/4			
W29	41.7	53^{4}	56^{7}	53^{4}	56^{7}		4 3/8					
T30	48.4	58	58^{3}	55^{7}	56^{3}		1 1/2			+		5^{7} T
JUL F1	31.6	56^{4}	59	56^{4}	59	1 7/8		5/8	0			
S2	25.1	59^{4}	60^{7}	59^{3}	60^{7}		4 7/8			4	8 3/4	
T5	34.0	60^{7}	60^{7}	58^{4}	59^{6}							4^{3}
W6	28.8	58^{2}	60^{2}	57^{6}	60	3/8		0	3/4			
T7	31.3	61	61^{6}	59	59^{6}		4					
F8	31.0	57^{1}	58^{2}	57	57^{4}							1/2
S9	10.5	57	58	56^{7}	57^{5}	1 3/8		0	1/8	4 1/2	4	
M11	28.3	57^{4}	58^{1}	55^{5}	55^{5}		1 1/4		1 1/4			
T12	37.6	55^{5}	59	55^{4}	59		7/8					2^{1} T

FAST UPWARD MOVEMENT

FIGURE 10

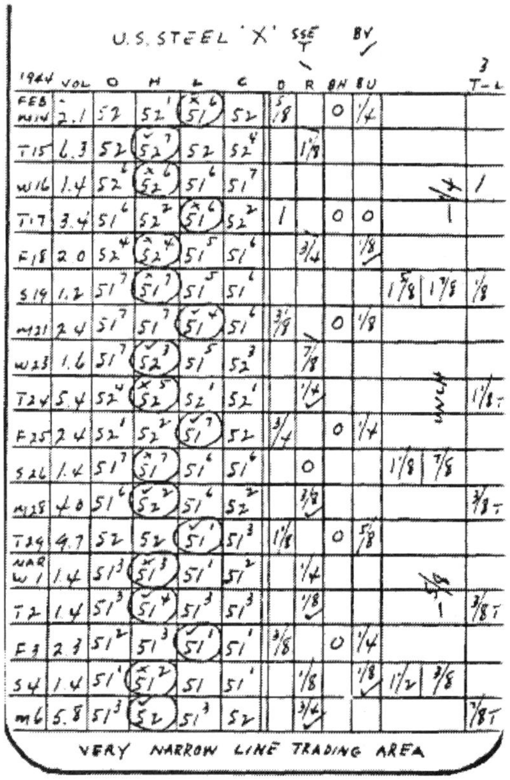

U.S. STEEL 'X' SSE BV

VERY NARROW LINE TRADING AREA

FIGURE 11

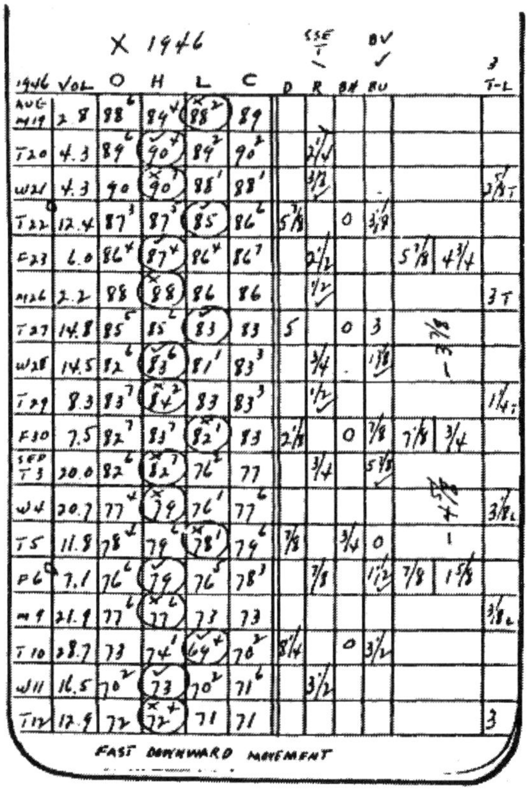

X 1946 SSE BV

FAST DOWNWARD MOVEMENT

FIGURE 12

COTTON JULY–51 NEW YORK

1950	O	H	L (3975)	C	D	R	BH	BU		T-L
SEP T 7	3986	4017	3985	3998		42			+72	
F 8	4051	4015	4000	4002		58				T 100
S 9	3997	4017	3984	4033	91		0	16	91 | 42	
M 11	4065	4070	4015	4017		86				
T 12	4003	4007	3975	3975						23
W 13	3965	3970	3930	3955	77		0	45	−28	
T 14	3990	4003	3961	4000		73				
F 15	4006	4034	3990	4019		21				90T
S 16	4016	4010	4005	4005	19		6	0	96 | 159	
M 18	3975	4004	3937	3937		0		68		
T 19	3955	3967	3945	3946						38
W 20	3938	3959	3930	3951	37		0	15	+6	
T 21	3955	4000	3955	3978		70				
F 22	3998	4018	3996	4011		18				88T
S 23	4006	4015	3995	4011	23		0	1	60 | 70	
M 25	4002	4009	3808	3980		14		187		
T 26	3973	3980	3956	3956						15
W 27	3960	3974	3933	3935	47		0	23	−136	
T 28	3950	3950	3901	3925		17		32		
F 29	3917	3982	3900	3910						1
S 30	3900	3900	3871	3875	61		0	29	108 | 31	
OCT M 2	3865	3935	3847	3924		64		24		
T 3	3955	3940	3906	3906		5				64T
W 4	3885	3923	3883	3905	57		0	23	+95	
T 5	3907	3957	3905	3951		74				
F 6	3970	4004	3955	3955		47				121
S 7	3960	3979	3958	3970	46		0	0	103 | 138	
M 9	3982	3985	3877	3877		27		81		
T 10	3876	3886	3838	3864						72
W 11	3750	3845	3750	3802	136		0	88	−216	
F 13	3802	3845	3785	3785		95				
S 14	3782	3783	3753	3754					136 | 122	32
M 16	3752	3782	3714	3726	68		0	39		
T 17	3723	3922	3722	3922		208				
W 18	3790	3888	3790	3825						174

DOWNTREND (HIGH TRADING AREA)

	O	H	L	C	D	R	BH	BU		T-L
T 19	3845	3875	3835	3845	53		0	0	+123	
F 20	3810	3850	3805	3834		15		30		
S 21	3846	3887	3845	3877		37			121 | 223	53T
M 23	3895	3910	3879	3884	8		23	0		
T 24	3904	3915	3894	3894		56				
W 25	3901	3905	3879	3901					+117	26
T 26	3908	3922	3903	3916	2		17	0		
F 27	3928	4028	3928	3980		125				
S 28	3995	4001	3982	3994					10 | 161	98
M 30	4000	4001	3950	3954	51		0	32		
T 31	3968	3984	3940	3955		34		10		
NOV W 1	3954	3980	3942	3942					−61	36
T 2	3948	3950	3901	3904	79		0	41		
F 3	3910	3939	3903	3930		38				
S 4	3944	3949	3933	3933		10			130 | 72	8T
M 6	3944	3960	3930	3930	19		11	3		
W 8	3935	3990	3918	3960		60		12	+162	
T 9	4160	4160	4052	4055		170				T 230
F 10	4070	4097	4066	4095	94		0	0	113 | 60	
M 13	4110	4147	4110	4122		87				
T 14	4128	4132	4110	4113						66
W 15	4120	4154	4114	4148	18		22	0	+91	
T 16	4156	4162	4136	4136		48				
F 17	4125	4183	4125	4176		21				64T
S 18	4190	4196	4176	4186	7		13	0	25 | 129	
M 20	4195	4219	4185	4215		43				
T 21	4193	4200	4169	4170						24
W 22	4172	4225	4170	4210	30		25	0	−46	
F 24	4202	4210	4100	4120		40		70		
S 25	4100	4140	4100	4140					30 | 83	30
M 27	4190	4232	4165	4168	0		92	0		
T 28	4210	4215	4106	4135		50		59		
W 29	4120	4162	4070	4105						32
T 30	4095	4138	4086	4095	76		0	0		
DEC F 1	4116	4133	4103	4129		47				

UPTREND (HIGH TRADING AREA)

FIGURE 13

SEASONAL TREND OF WHEAT PRICES

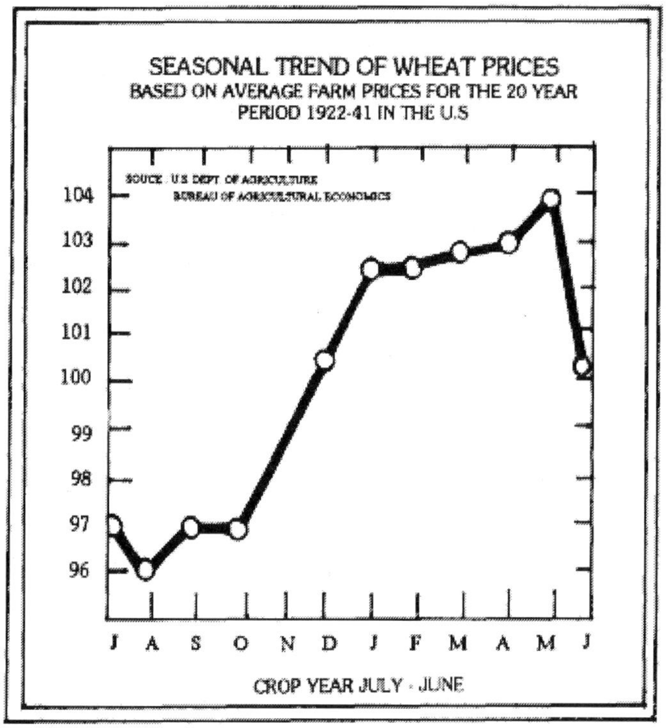

FIGURE 14

    The seasonal trend of wheat, as shown in the above chart shows the traditional pattern. Easy prices prevail at harvest time, but once the pressure of the harvest is over, the price level starts to work higher until it is again time for the new crop to be received.

    The downturn usually occurs about one month prior to the harvest. While this pattern has not necessarily held true during recent years of high loans and high prices, it could become more active when the loan may become effective in diminishing free supplies.

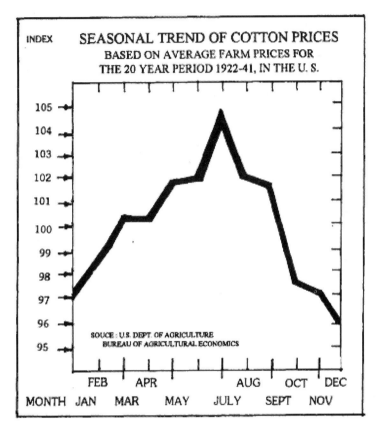

FIGURE 15

Here is a pattern that can be relied upon by both the [trader] and the speculator—the speculator who is familiar with seasonal movements can take advantage of these trading opportunities.

SEASONAL TREND OF CORN PRICES

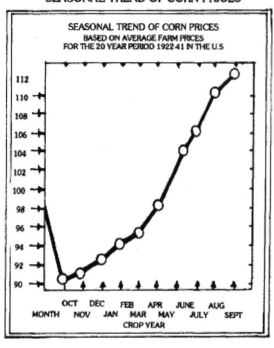

FIGURE 16

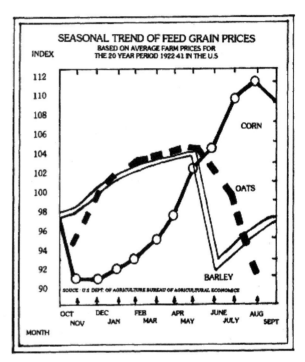

FIGURE 17

Historically, corn values follow a distinct seasonal pattern. From a low in November—the peak of the harvest movement—farm prices move higher each month until they reach their peak about the following August when remaining supplies of the old crop are scarce.

After August, prices generally ease in anticipation of new crop supplies.

While the seasonal longer up-trend is from the low in November to a high in August, this line is broken into numerous trading rallies and declines and these are the short term Trading Areas.

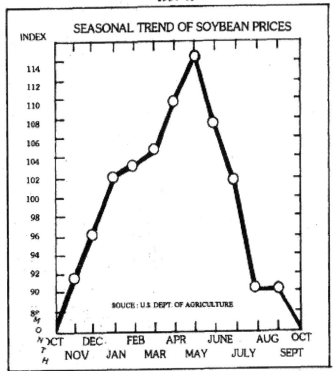

SEASONAL TREND OF SOYBEAN PRICES
BASED ON AVERAGE FARM PRICES FOR
1937-41

FIGURE 18

Look at the accompanying Seasonal Trend Chart, depicting the normal trend of soybean prices during a crop year, based on the years 1937/41. By about May or June, when their price declines again, most crushers' needs have been satisfied and a fairly accurate idea of the remaining crop-year's needs have been formed. In anticipation of next year's crop, the price index begins to decline but before harvest time it levels off slightly. Then comes the weight of the harvest that forces prices still lower. Crushers, in order to ensure themselves of an adequate year round supply, purchase about 50% of the crop before December 31. The price level accordingly moves steadily and sharply upward from the October lows as the demand for beans is being filled. Both the [trader] and the speculator should take advantage of these seasonal price savings.Here is a pattern that can be relied upon by both the [trader] and the speculator—the speculator who is familiar with seasonal movements can take advantage of these trading opportunities.

CHAPTER 12
LIMIT DAY MOVES

The beginning of a series of Downward Limit Moves must start from a comparatively high range of prices.

We have Three (3) Selling Days, the Selling Day Objective, the Short Sale Objective and the high made FIRST on a Buying Day, but only two of these objectives could be used The Short Sale Day, and the Buying Day High made FIRST, in a downward movement.

The Beginning of this movement must start from one of these three tops, therefore, should this decline take place from a Selling Day Objective, we of course, would be out of the market by virtue of having sold our long stock at this point. In this case we would be without an indication to reenter the market, with the result that we would miss the move, however, being out of the market at this time carries [its] own compensation by reason of conserving our resources and the anticipation of the increased buying power at much lower prices.

This in itself is one of the fundamentals of speculation—to be able to protect your capital and be in a position to act on a more favorable opportunity when it comes along.

A movement of this kind starting from a Short Sale Objective would put us in and being a limit move, we would stay in, first because we are speculators and secondly, "because we may not be able to get out".

The movement starting from the high made FIRST on a Buying Day, is also, generally a Short Sale Objective and were we in such a move it would become apparent, at once, for it would reach and run through the Short Sale Day Low—the low of the day before—a Buying Day Objective but the apparent lack of rally here would prove the move as out of the ordinary and one of our rules would come into play "On a Buying Day when a stock or future shows no tendency to rally and looks like it will close 'flat', that is, the low and close at the same price, it usually goes lower". In a move of this kind the closing prices are generally right on the bottom eighth, we do not buy long stock, for when the Low is made LAST the Buying Day Circle would have a check (√) in it, indicating a lower trend.

The starting of a series of Upward Limit Moves must start from a comparatively low range—perhaps restricted prices—or be the culminating move after a long slow rising market.

This movement would generally start from a Buying Day Objective or from a Violation of a Buying Day Low made FIRST or from a low on a Short Sale Day, from an active, severe 'sell off' from the Short Sale Day High. When this happens the decline is more or less panicky with each price change going lower until it reaches a bottom and then the turn about is abrupt and the rally is very active and fast with the gains usually held but sometimes followed by a decline from this rally and while the first low may not be reached—the next day, the Buying Day—the real start of the upward move would take place from the Higher Bottom on the Buying Day.

This rally would start when the market had the appearance of going lower and with a general bearish atmosphere. Some specific news usually causes the start of this move and the technical position of the market is ready to be influenced by it. The manipulator would only start this move after a strong technical position had been built up through too many unwise short positions and the way to get an extended short position in the market is to make it look weak and have the traders sell it short at or near the bottom.

We have no way of knowing when a move of this kind might start but we have two chances to get aboard in the Upward move—the Buying Day Low and the Violation of the Buying Day Low made FIRST—should the turn come on either of these days. In the Downward move we have the Short Sale Day and the Buying Day High made FIRST.

CHAPTER 13
THE THREE DAY TRADING METHOD

PART 1

With the selection of the stock, it is only good judgment to get a report on the company, its past and future probabilities—but unless the market action of the stock confirms the report a trader should let it alone—watch but don't buy. The time for buying should be based solely on the technical indications and the present market position, in relation to the low and high for the year. It could be selling so near to a top (Temporarily, perhaps), that by waiting a short time it can be bought at a wide concession. Most all Bull markets show at least one or more important declines during the year that are buying opportunities, but the most important part is; starting at exactly the right time. A decline in a stock, due to a general decline in the market as a whole, is not of great concern but the way it acts on the rally, and the preparations for a new move is important. A trader should look for buying in a stock around the lows of important declines—after the market stabilizes. It takes considerable buying to start a stock up and continuous buying to keep it going up. (Many good stocks lack trading appeal, sponsorship, or due to other conditions, move with such sluggish action that they are unattractive to the more active traders.)

Stocks with a good future potential should be watched but a trader should not wait until 'they make the news' before buying—at this time they might be a better sale. Buying in a stock shows, in the way the stock acts. He should follow the progress of a stock at bottoms or where it begins to form a well defined horizontal trend—confined to a narrow trading range—and trades on a fair amount of volume and activity, with some fair size lots of stock. He then waits for a day of unusual activity and volume and gets ready to buy at the very inception of the 'break-out' of this range, top side. He will buy part of his stock at this point—then wait for a reaction to see how it acts on this decline and to confirm his judgment, whether he was right in buying the first lot. He then buys more after the stock rallies and just as it makes a new high. His buying is done in this manner, Because: At times, the stock may turn and go in the opposite direction, and may 'dip' low enough to break to line of lows at the bottom of this range. (An action of this kind 'cleans up all the stops' below the line of bottom prices and 'shakes off' a following before the real move gets under way.) Having acquired his stock he holds on for the move; an indefinite period, perhaps three to six months or longer, or until he recognizes the described action around tops.

In some years and at other times, some stocks and commodities, begin their advance from other than trading ranges. Bottoms of long declines may be reached by a particular violent downward thrust—establish a low—generally followed by an immediate sharp rally and a subsequent slower decline on greatly reduced volume and activity—stopping short of the last low. A trader does not try to buy long stock on this fast decline—he waits for the 'quiet spot' on the reaction after the rally—and when the market becomes 'dull'. He will buy part of his line at this point (with the intent to sell out should the stock make a new low) then add to it where the stock begins to make new highs in series. In case he is forced to sell, he starts over again from a new low—using this same action. (The manner of buying at bottoms—shows why—he should not expect to get less than a 10% average above extreme lows.)

A stock that trades in a listless manner on very small volume; with intermittent small transactions, with absent days of trading, shows neglect; and no immediate interest, and should not be bought until it shows a more active participation in the market. A trader recognizing this action in a stock should look to the company report for the reason. A stock must be traded in fair size lots and volume in order to accumulate it. (This action can, also be seen in the commodities markets, in the distant futures, for a short time after the 'start of trading' in them.)

Experienced traders and tape readers can generally distinguish a rally from a change in trend by figuring how far a stock should come back, allowing that a normal rally is from one-half to two-thirds of the decline. In case the decline is not over, the rally will fall short. The large transactions will be on the downside and the smaller lots on the upside. The volume is light and the activity 'fades away' with the rally 'dying out' at the top. Where the trend is to continue the trading shows a steady rise on increasing volume and demand for the stock, and where there is an urgent demand for stock for 'short covering' the pace will be accelerated. The large transactions are on the upside and are taken at the higher prices, with the smaller transactions on the downside. (This same action can be seen in the smallest daily—in the broader and longer movements—and in the Market Averages.)

Many stocks make two tops—the Real and Actual—the Real top is where the first heavy liquidation takes place after long advances; then, after a decline of a week or more, a rally or continuation of the advance, many times, will exceed the first high making the Actual top on a volume as large—more or less. A trader should be on the alert to begin his selling the instant he detects this inside selling. (The point here is: he must sell when he has a market, if his holdings are large.) Experienced traders take their profits at this point and do not try to anticipate an Actual Top. (Which may or may not happen.) The high made on this kind of action may be one and the same—the Real and Actual. When this does happen the stock makes a new high and has a tendency to make the ordinary traders intensely bullish—they continue to 'hold on' or 'come in' as new buyers—to take the stock at, perhaps, top prices. (And this is just what is expected of them.)

The Real Top, is generally one or several days of advancing prices after a long move up, culminating with a quick, sharp, upward thrust on abnormally large volume and activity, compared to previous trading. The stock makes a high then resists all further buying—the supply and demand comes into balance—with the trading very active and sustained—but the stock makes little or no progress either way. The heavy selling at this point is, temporarily discontinued, but the 'selling sources' continue to force a little more stock on the market than can be absorbed, without loss, causing this sagging decline, on greatly reduced daily volume. Near or at the low of this decline there is a noticeable increase in the volume for a day or more—the stock must be bought in large enough quantities to absorb all selling and turn the stock up. The day of heaviest support is the Real Bottom, then, many times after a short sub-normal rally or series of rallies, the stock will sell just a little lower on a negligible amount of volume—making the Actual Bottom—before the rally or uptrend is resumed. (A new high has a bullish effect and causes buying. A new low has a bearish effect and causes traders to sell out at bottoms, or at least, refrain from buying.)

A trader will repurchase a small part of his stock 'as a trading lot' on this decline in anticipation of a rally or on the assumption that an uptrend will extend far enough to make a new and Actual Top. (But, with the firm resolve to re-sell at, thru, and above on this new high—or to 'get out quick'—if after a rally, the reaction breaks the last or support low.)

There are other stocks that make one top—the Real and Actual—and on comparatively light volume, with no signs indicating that a top has been reached. The long decline starts with a series of small reactions and rallies but with a definite downward tendency. These tops are difficult to recognize. (If, in fact, they can be.) A trader should understand the characteristics of these stocks or at least have some idea of the percentage appreciation or number of points in the swings of the past years, as a guide to the future—and he should be satisfied to sell, if and when, past results as good or better can be attained. In this case a stock that fails to make a new high in a reasonable period of time should be sold, particularly so, if other stocks in the market are showing the heavy top action. (The trader who can recognize these diverse movements in the market can use them as confirmation of the weakened technical condition of the market as a whole).

A trader who will start right—buy and sell according to these 'age old' tenets—will find little need for many of these 'new discoveries' and other 'wearisome' statistical market indices.

PART 2

This method of trading is applicable of both—Grains, Commodities and Stock on the 'Big Board", however, in applying this method to stocks, select only those stocks that appear on the tape every day and with large volume, relative to the daily transactions of the whole market and which are the public trading favorites, the bid and ask is not so wide and they are easier to buy and sell.

Low priced stocks will not do for they do not have wide enough fluctuations.

Many of the stocks that made up the Dow-Jones Averages are good fluctuating stocks and they move over a two or three points or more range, during this swing. Of course, there are many others and they can be found in the Forty to Seventy Five Dollar price range that are applicable to this method.

First select a few stocks and make up a book on them—you can usually get the back number newspapers at the public libraries.

Start your book from the low point of any Secondary Reaction in the market or at least go back a few months, so that you will have some of the past action of the stock to study, then study the stocks you decide to trade in, observe the way they rally and decline and the number of points in the spreads from highs to lows to highs, study them for regularity and continuity of their movements. All this information you can get from your book after you make it up.

All stock have certain characteristics of their own, in the way they move, some rally ahead of the market, some with the market, while others fluctuate 'Up and Down and Up and Down in a series of rallies and declines' they just seem to 'plug' their way along. This last type is good for our trading purpose, if they, also, trade with a spread wide enough for buying and selling with profit.

After you have found a good trading stock, stay with it and forget about the others and what they are doing.

This method is purely mechanical, in [its] strictest sense, but you must develop a certain confidence in [its] movements, for knowing how it has recorded the movement in the past, you can feel reasonably certain that it will preserve this same movement in the future and used in this sense, you need not invoke the finer points of trading, as you would do in using the daily trading method.

This method is based on the greater percentage of gains over losses, for you will have loss swings, but the records show that generally, but with few exceptions, the loss swings in points are small and the profit swings, with a few exceptions, are large, but the profit swings in points must of a necessity outnumber the loss points in an up trend, therefore, when consistently following this simpler method of trading—that of Buying and Selling as advantageously as possible, as the Buying and Selling Objectives appear, the method is profitable in the long run—your profits are made on balance.

The above is well for the long side of the market but we want to take advantage of the short side, too, for this is half the profits, however, selling short, stocks on the 'Big Board' is a little different matter than when selling short on the Commodity Markets, on account of a Stock Exchange ruling which restricts short sales to some extent. Both with the Three Day Method and the Daily Trading, we many times hit the top price, when selling, even to the top eighth, so in this case with stocks, we may not be able to 'get off' a short sale as we could do with a commodity, where there are no restrictions on short selling.

After a stock gets up to a high or where

distribution starts it enters another trading range, the same as near the low point, only that this range will be wider with many fluctuations up and down, with activity and volume, in order to distribute it, therefore it might be well to wait for this kind of action before trading it on the short side. The past records show that the long side is profitable without short sales and many traders can not or will not sell stocks short. Trading with this method he can take his choice.

The above is not written to keep you from selling short, for should the stock you select to trade in, develop enough spread on these swings so that you can trade it both ways, do so, for you are trading and are 'there' to accept any gains the market offers you, no matter in what stage of the movement nor on what side, long or short.

In using this method the Selling Day Objective is eliminated, however, always watch the trend of prices on this day, for you can usually get a forecast of what to expect the next day—the Short Sale Day, your Selling Day—and you will want to know if your Selling Objective will be on a penetration or whether the price will 'fall short' of the Objective.

On the Selling Day watch the high and low and which was made FIRST or LAST, the high on this day being made LAST is generally a good sign that the opening will be up and your Selling Objective—the high of Selling Day will be penetrated.

When the high of Selling Day is made FIRST and the close is up from the low after a reaction, the probabilities favor a further rally and a penetration for your Selling Objective—but having bought your stock on a Buying Day Low and to then get a Violation of the Buying Day Low—next day—the price generally 'falls short' of your Selling Objective—this action is a good forecast of a failure to penetrate and it shows a weak uptrend and it generally occurs in a Downward Trading Area—so don't expect too much at your Selling Objective. On the other hand when the Buying Day Low holds, the forecast is for a larger gain and penetration of your Selling Day Objective and this Objective is the high reached on the Short Sale Day.

At your Selling Objective you must sell out, either way, with a profit or loss on the penetration or as near to it, on the failure to penetrate. DO NOT HOLD ON OR CARRY YOUR STOCK DOWN.

The next day being a Buying Day you will probably get an opportunity to buy your stock at a lower price with the chances of making up any loss, in case this happened to be one of those days swings and with a profit besides, on your next trade.

It might be well to point out here that a trader must take losses but he takes them when they are small and he tries to stop them as quickly as possible when he sees that he is wrong and in taking them he is not losing anything at all but is playing for position and a more favorable chance to trade that he knows will soon appear.

The Violation of the Buying Day Low does not change your Selling Objective as it does when using the daily method—you do your buying on a Buying Day and hold on, even though, this low is violated—you ride through this reaction and wait for your Selling Objective which is the penetration or failure to penetrate the Selling Day High on a Short Sale Day.

You are using this method as a purely mechanical way of trading—you buy and sell and figure your profits on balance of greater gains over losses, over the longer term swing in stocks and during the life of a grain or commodity future.

A trader using this three day method for grain futures will find that during the life of any of them he has approximately One Hundred Opportunities or trading swings on the long side, plus an equal amount on the short side from the starting to the expiration dates and that the past records show that over (50%) of the Buying and Selling Objectives were accomplished on penetrations at these points.

The trends in the markets vary from year to year in that some Bull and Bear Markets will be achieved by a series of wide trading moves both in the Primary swings and in the Secondaries, while in other years the swings will be a series of narrow persistent upward and downward movements. Look at the charts on stocks of the past years and then make up a book of their movements during these different kinds of trends.

A trader has a fairly reliable guide on the kind of reaction trend to expect by noting the type of upward movement that preceded it. Had this uptrend been accomplished by a fast and almost vertical climb, he would expect the reaction trend to be of the same nature, perhaps a precipitous decline. Had the trader been using the Three Day Method he would forego buying on the Buying Objective and would wait for the Short Sale Day—then sell short—covering the sale on the Buying Day—and again selling on the Short Sale Day, until after the urgency of the decline was over and the stock began to receive support of the kind from which trading rallies began to take place, after the declines. He would then begin to use his Buying Day Objective again and buy and sell as he did before.

Since the intent of the reaction is to get the price down, buying long stock at any stage is going against the trend but few reactions have ever been completed in one straight drop, therefore, we have found that at certain stages of the reaction it is profitable to buck the trend and play both sides of the market and this stage of the reaction is after the heat of the selling is over and the stock begins to trade around the low point.

The same can be said of the fast upward movement for when prices are low—in a period of congestion or accumulation—the movement may start with a fast mark up of prices and this action usually takes place from some kind of restricted trading area—the intent then is to get the price higher, without a following, so that any reaction of the daily kind will be small in most cases, too small, and fast to trade both ways. The trader then would use the Buying Day Objective and let the short side alone. He would buy on the Buying Days and hold on until the Short Sale Day, then sell and buy back again on the Buying Day. After the stock or commodity began to show trading declines from the higher prices he would then begin to use his Short Sale Objective.

The Up or Down Movement made on wide daily rallies and declines should be traded both ways.

The consistent buying and selling through trends of all kinds does work out in favor of the trader over the longer term, yet a trader need not make his plays this way and it is not advised that he do so, at least not if he expects the market to run into one of these fast moves, either way.

These loss day swings can be very severe and they look more formidable while they are happening and it takes more courage than most traders have to 'ride out' these moves, even though, the greater part of the loss may be on paper and only temporary but it does require considerable more money to finance them.

CHAPTER 14
THE INVESTOR AND SWING TRADER

The Investor and Swing Trader, has a means of accumulation and distribution in the use of the Three Day Method.

In buying for accumulation it is not wise to try to buy a full line all at one time. The same for selling—even, though each would like to liquidate all at once—there are times when it can't be done, the market is not technically strong enough to take the selling and by trying to do so, he may get a price far less than would suit him.

By applying the Buying Day Objective to his accumulation and the Selling Day Objectives to his distribution, he could save himself many points—and dollars.

The Investor or Swing Trader is in no different position than the Daily trader—he too, should make up a book on the stocks he intends to buy and sell. Both would first determine the kind of market—Bull or Bear—and the price position of the stock, in relation to the market as a whole and either buying or selling would have to be initiated on the minor trend—the daily price fluctuations—regardless of the longer term trend—and both would try to buy as advantageously as possible consistent with a Bull Movement.

Suppose the line was to be 500 shares or more—each would use the Buying Day—observing the conditions around the Buying Day Objective—an order would be placed for part, say, 100 shares, after getting them he would then wait until the next Buying Day and place an order for another lot, continuing in this manner until he had bought his full line. This procedure would be a higher average cost but each lot would be more apt to show a profit and the trader would have some assurance that he was following a rising trend.

Had he started his buying during a comparatively low range of prices and was in a rising market, it is not likely that he would be forced to carry a heavy load at a loss, in case of a sudden decline in the whole market.

At the determined time for selling, he would use the same procedure, he would sell only on a Selling Objective—the Short Sale Day and the Buying Day High made FIRST. In this manner he would be liquidating his stock on a rising trend.

In either case, the trader would have some assurance that he was getting or trying to get, the best prices at the time of his buying or selling.

Trading technique, is simply the ability through study, observation and experience, to detect the manipulation that takes place in the markets at all times, and to recognize the signals in each, of the several phases, of the market movement. The most important consideration for speculation, even ahead of earnings and dividends, is the technical position of the stock in relation to the market as a whole— leading or trailing—its position within its own group—leading or trading—and the group attention in the news—at this writing it is television.

Swing traders and semi-investors are more concerned with price appreciation, therefore, selection of a stock is of the utmost importance. Most of the stocks that make up the back-bone of the market are in the conservative class and trading profits should be figured on a percentage basis and not on points. The trader who will do a little retrospective research will find that many stocks he may have in mind are not suitable for his style of trading. Get the highs and lows of the one or more sustained swings that a stock makes each year and then figure the percentage gains and losses of the rally and decline swings, from lows to highs and highs to lows. The Market Averages may show great gains and losses up and down, in points, with the per cent gain or loss of an individual stock disappointingly small.

A trader buying stocks around any low point,

Bear Bottoms or Secondary Reactions in a Bull Market (here he should use the 3 day rule for accumulation) should carefully check the percentage rise of his stock as the price moves up from the low point but most important: a stock that is going up will do so with but small and normal set-backs until it reaches the high of the move, regardless of percentages, so the trader must be constantly on the alert for the day when his stock will make top—in many cases this top will be made quite unexpectedly but not without warning. Watch the build-up of the volume for a few days prior to the top and the greatly reduced volume the next and for a few days after or the volume might remain large for a few days before and after the high is made. The decrease in volume is caused by a let-up in the selling pressure for technically the stock may not be able to withstand further heavy selling without breaking the price, too much. Many times a trading range is formed between the high and the low of the break-back and the stock will trade in this range indefinitely, weeks and months, depending on the strength or weakness of the general market—further distribution takes place in this range and on the way down, if, the general market is headed that way. This phenomenon of the action of individual stocks is a feature of the market prior to bull market endings—with one stock after another refusing to participate in any further rise in the market, while the general market continues to advance—this same action takes place in a lesser degree before severe intermediate declines. This may not be the action of low priced late movers, that move up fast, make a top and start to decline, seldom going back to their highs a second time. Being behind, they must hustle to catch up with the general market which is plainly showing a declining tendency. This sudden reaching of a top on greatly increased volume compared with the previous daily totals, then, a slight break of several percent of price from the high while the volume continues large, is the results of heavy selling, mixed with public buying and inside short selling, caused perhaps by advance information adversely affecting the stock—sufficient to cause large profit taking or the price

is deemed high enough to begin distribution of the stock. Regardless of the reason, this action definitely warns the trader that the intent is not to put the price higher, at least not for the present—and is his signal to unload—the market is broad enough at these times to take the selling and is the opportune time to turn paper profits into cash.

The low points of Bull Market Secondary Reactions are just the reverse of the top action, the low many times is made on relatively heavy volume, then a rally for a day or two and a further decline on very light volume with the price holding above the last low point, with trading dull (established points at either highs or lows may be penetrated slightly by the trading that takes place but are not sufficient reason to withhold selling or buying at these points). The short seller on this trend must be on the alert for this same big day, only on the downside: for then the stock is in supply for covering short sales and is the long stock bought at higher prices, now, being sold at the bottom.

The market action for a swing trading is identically the same as that used for the 3 day method, only on an enlarged scale. The minor movement receives the same support on the declines and is subjected to the same pressure on the rallies.

CHAPTER 15
PERTINENT POINTS

The rallies and declines of the past movements in stocks, commodities and grains—meet support and supply at or near these Objectives, study them and watch the price action on the 'tape'.

Do some paper trading—try buying and selling for about Ten (10) Days, until you get the 'feel' of the market. You are not day dreaming by doing this nor are you reading the prices after the close of the market, with exultations or recriminations of what might have been, had you done this or that.

Take a pad and pencil with you to market, then buy and sell by using these Objectives. Check yourself with the record after a couple of weeks of this kind of practice.

This trading practice will teach self control, curb impetuous buying and selling, control your patience and cause you to keep in mind all the actions that can take place at these Buying and Selling Objective Points.

Never try to anticipate the market farther ahead than your signals, 'cinch' your profits as the market gives them to you, don't hold on past a signal because a trend looks strong or you think the price will go higher or lower, it may do exactly as you think and does many times but your 'play' is to take what the market offers you and at the exact time of this offering.

Don't think about any other Objective, only the immediate one, that is, if you are looking for a Buying Objective, think only about the action that can happen around this point.

Never make a trade unless it favors your 'play', it is better to pass up the entire trading session than to buy or sell on a guess that it will turn out all right, wait, until you are reasonably sure and the market many times makes it very plain, when to buy or sell. The best practice you can get is to go to the public library and get the past quotations of the daily transactions on a commodity or stock and while making up

a book on them, observe the repetitious action of the daily price changes and you will get the 'swing and feeling' of the regular rhythm of this action and note the similarity of movement in all of them—past and present.

Watch the low and close of each day and how and where they closed, near the high for the day or near or at the low for the day and for what action and forecast for the next day. Be prepared for wide openings up or down, particularly if prices are up or down (10) points or more, which could be the top or bottom of a Trading Area. Many times the opening price will be your Buying or Selling Objective on a penetration or failure to penetrate.

The commodities markets being seasonal affairs have and will continue to have broad swings with activity and deeper penetrations at the Objectives, in the Trading Areas and these are the profit making moves.

Forget about a trade after you have made it, if you didn't get the last eighth or if the price went higher after you sold or lower after you covered your short sale.

Keep in mind the tactics used around the important turning points—Objectives—and keep looking forward to your next trade. Remember, you are trading for quick, small but sure profits and this is exactly how a floor trader looks at the business. Take what the market offers you at the time and don't hold on for what you think the market should do, trade the market on what it does. In daily trading you will have enough opportunities to keep you busy and should you find it, too, trying [to] use the Three Day Method for a change.

A trader should make up a book on several of the grain options and on a few stocks, then study them for their movements. After deciding on the one he intends to trade in, take only that book to market with him, or at most two books, one for Short Sale Objective and the other for Buying

Objective. In the beginning this eliminates a lot of confusion by watching or trying to watch them all, for as one option moves, the others will usually be in line.

After making up several books on the grains and stocks, he will find that some of them will differ, in that one may be at a Buying Objective while another a Sale or Short Sale but this is the continuity so follow them that way.

There is nothing inconsistent with this so far as the trader is concerned, as an example: A trader may have a book on two Wheat Futures, Corn or Soybeans—the same with stocks—one a buy and one a short sale on the same day. Now, on this same day and before the opening, if the trader has not already done so, he will review the market of the previous day on both the Buy and Short Sale Options and will note the signal mark for the possible trend in each.

He then expects an up or down opening he watches for either. On the up opening he watches for the Short Sale option to reach the Short Sale Objective—that of selling through the Sale Day High—if so, this would be the trade to make, a short sale—for it would be happening first. On an action of this kind his Buy Day Option or stock will probably be in line with all the others and it, too, would probably be up—we know that a reaction generally takes place from a high made FIRST on a Buying Day, so he would watch it but would not buy it for awhile. Now, should the opening be down, it would be making the low FIRST for his Buying Option, so this would be the trade to receive first attention.

On a Buying Day, buy at or below the low of the previous day, unless the market looks like it might close on the low for the day. Failure to rally from a 'sell off'.

When the low and close are about the same on a Short Sale Day, we usually get our (BU) Buy Under, the price goes lower, next day.

Watch how the Objectives are made—FIRST or LAST—Objectives made FIRST are the surest and quickest for profits.

Watch the close to determine the extent of rally when Buying Day Low is being made LAST—a 'flat' closing generally means a Violation—next day—and when made FIRST are usually good

buying 'spots' for a quick profit.

A purchase on a Buying Day must show a profit in the spread, from low to closing price—when the low and close is about the same price or where the gain at close is lost on the opening of Selling Day, sell out on any rally towards your Buying Day Low point.

Watch the range from high to low on a Short Sale Day, to determine the possible low point at which to buy, next day—the Buying Day.

Having 'put out' a short sale on a Short Sale Day, then if the stock reacts and the spread is very wide—cover your sale the same day—this profit will help reduce the costs, in case, the next day, being a Buying Day you may have to buy at a Higher Bottom. This is caused by a rally before the close of the Short Sale Day and makes the Buying Day Low, higher. Buying a Higher Bottom is usually profitable.

When the Buying Day Low is Violated, the high for the movement is usually made on the next Buying Day—3 day swing—it is usually safer to pass up the Short Sale Day, if it looks like the high might be made LAST and try to sell short on the high of Buying Day made FIRST, but 'cover' your sale the same day. This gives you both a short sale and a buy, but 'cover' the short when you have a profit and wait for the best chance to 'go long'. This action usually happens in an Uptrend Trading Area—Downtrend Areas, give you lower tops and bottoms.

The amount of rally from a Buying Day Low to the close, determines the action for the Selling Objective, as weak or strong, unless it [is] one of those days where you get all the range on the same day, then the opening on the Selling Day, is liable to be down.

The decline from a Selling Day High, may cause the price to go under the previous low—Buying Day Low—which will show the Short Sale Objective as being weak, if the High on Selling Day was made FIRST and the close is somewhere near the low of the day.

On a Buying Day, after a decline, should the rally from the low be active and strong and the price carry up to and through the previous high—Short Sale Day—sell out your stock before the close, for many times this will be the high and the opening of Selling Day may be down—this is the reverse of the wide decline on the Short Sale Day, where you 'cover' in the same session on a wide decline. In either case the market is giving you a good profit without much delay—why take chances on losing part of it?

In the Downtrend Areas, both the Sale and Short Sale Objectives, generally 'fall short' of penetrations—the Buying Day Low is usually Violated.

- When the Decline unit is small, the Rally unit is usually large.

- When the Decline unit is large, the Rally unit is usually small.

- When the low on a Buying Day is higher than the high of the previous day—Short Sale Day—you have a Decline Zero and a forecast of a rally.

- When the Decline Zero appears the rally is usually profitable.

- The amount of rally from a Short Sale Day Low, plus a higher opening on a Buying Day causes the Decline Zero.

- The lack of rally from a Buying Day Low, plus a down opening on a Selling Day causes the Rally Zero and a forecast of nearby lower prices.

- The Rally Zero always violates the Buying Day Low.

There seems to be about two swings a week, one Upward and one Downward. In the Bull movement, the one downward will be longer and is the swing that causes the failures to penetrate the Selling Objectives and the cause of Buying Day Low Violations.

When trading on the Three Day Method—buy on a Buying Day and sell out on a Short Sale Day—when the previous Buying Day Low is not violated expect greater gains—when this violation occurs the gains are usually small and may even show a loss for the swing. Having bought on the Buying Day, you must hold on through this violation but, also, you must sell out on the Short Sale Day, but expect your profits to be small on account of a failure to penetrate your Selling Objective. Rallies don't always fail to reach the Selling Objective but generally they do so. Don't hold on too long, when you get a profit take it and don't expect too much, in this case.

Use the Three Day Method for the accumulation of stocks and commodities but don't buy your full line all at one time—buy part of your line only on a Buying Day and then another part on the next Buying Day, etc. Where a Buying Day Low may be Violated—don't buy at all, but having bought (here you may have bought on the low for the day and the stock rallied but began to sell off near the close) and the stock looks like it may close on the low for the day—sell out your last purchase before the close and let the market alone until your next Buying Day. The reasoning here is, that Violations begin to show up in downtrends and downtrends are not the kind for accumulation.

In selling out a line at higher prices use only the Selling Days—preferably the Short Sale and the Buying Day High made FIRST—in the case of the Violation of last Buying Day, it is reasonable to look for a high of the swing on the next Buying Day—many times this high will be made LAST, in this case it is a strong 'spot' for selling long stock.

Since all trends in commodities are seasonal watch the position of your future and whether it is up or down and in what month. The months when they normally sell at their highest and lowest points.

At times, during the last few days before an option expires, the technical position of the market may cause several wide rallies and declines, during the same session—take your profit at the first opportunity—complete your trade, depending on the kind of trading Objective you are using—then stay out of the market—don't try to trade these rallies and declines—they are aimless whip-saw movement and they don't favor your play.

The price you pay at the time of buying and selling has nothing to do with it—the point is to determine the correct place for buying or selling. In the Uptrend you continue to buy and sell on a rising range of prices. In the Downtrend you do the same on a declining range of prices.

When accumulation is taking place in a stock, considerable buying would be done around a low point for a considerable period of time, then when the floating supply is about bought up in and around this range of low prices, the price will move up to a higher range for further buying—when accumulation is completed at the lower and higher ranges—then the stock is in position for [its] upward move, for a top and distribution.

Professional traders usually cover around old lows and sell out around the highs. At the lows the stock is in supply and it gives them a chance to cover short sales. At the tops the stock is in demand and it gives them a market for long stock and short sales.

Until a trader gains in experience, he should buy and sell just as his Objectives are reached—put in your order to buy or sell just as soon as the price appears on the tape and many times your buying or selling 'spot' will be at or shortly after the opening. Those traders who use charts in their work may find them of use in conjunction with this method of trading, If so, well and good—those traders who go in for astrology and statistics to a point where they can tell you "the rate of growth on a corn stalk in one night's pull of the moon", might, also, ask themselves, If the 'boy' on the floor who makes the market understands these theories. Perhaps not, and cares less, however, he does understand how the markets of the past were made and how well they worked and is not losing much sleep trying to alter or devise a new way—not so much that it can be noticed over the past 100 years.

A trader with any method or system of trading must develop and have a certain amount of confidence in it—with this means of trading he must believe in the occurrence and recurrence of the past pattern of movements. The intent has been to keep the method as simple as possible and to rely on the fact that at these trading Objectives, a trader can buy and sell with a profit. Use it in [its] most mechanical form and stay away from production and marketing statistics, if possible, for in short term trading, the trader is concerned, only, with the day to day price changes—the spreads between the Buying and Selling Objectives.

Soybeans have a very promising future as a trading vehicle—they are a useful and minority crop—and it would be an astonishing revelation to the trader who will go back and make up a book and a record of the fluctuations for the years 1948-49-50.

It is not within the scope of this book to cover in detail all commodities—it is sufficient to point out that the 'tape' action, the rise and fall of prices in the market, is the same for all. A book is made up and traded in exactly the same way by those traders who want to trade in cotton, fats and oils or any other commodity that has a continuous daily price change on the 'tape' or frequently posted price changes.

ADDITIONAL MATERIAL

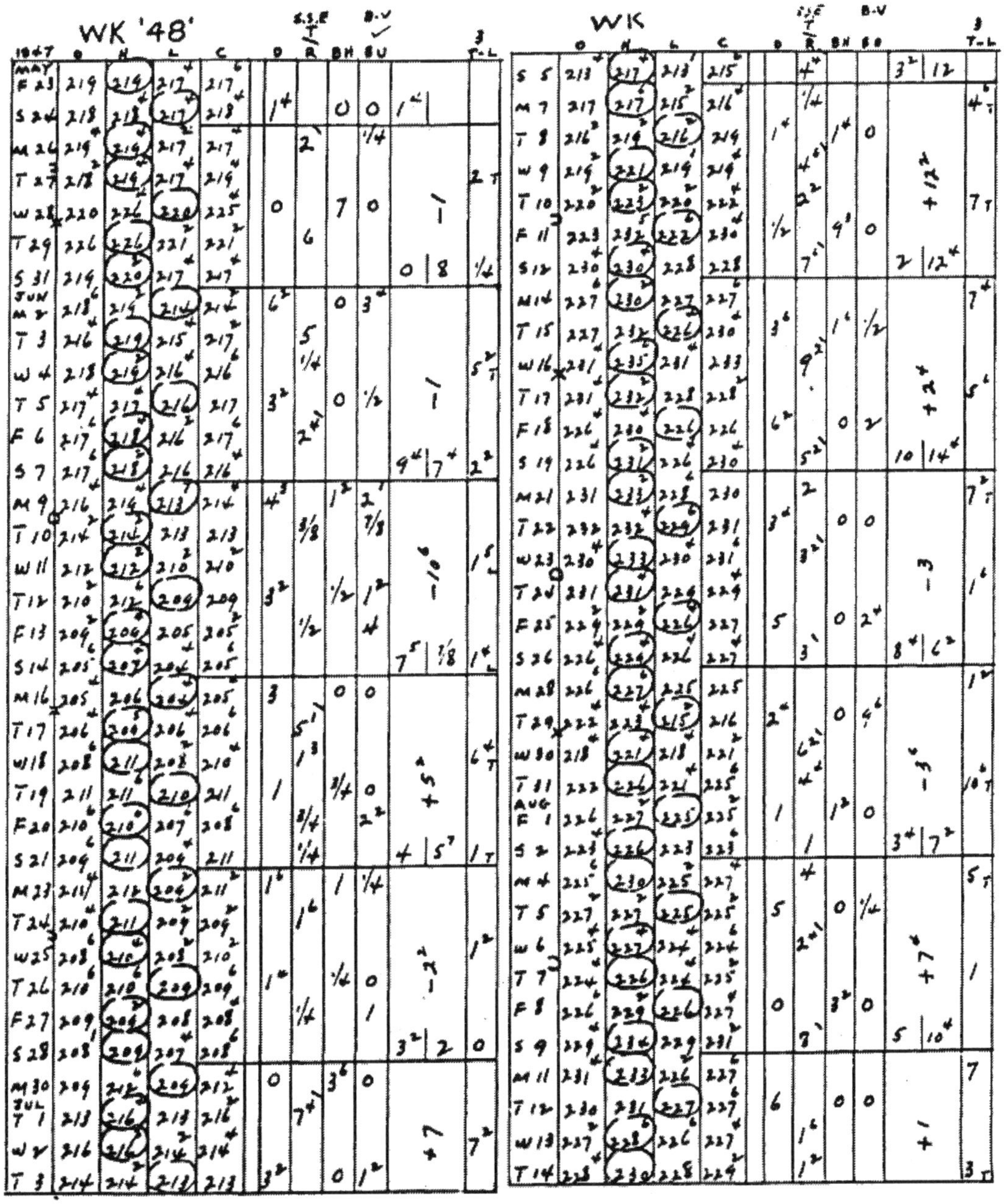

FIGURES

Left table — WK '48

1947	O	H	L	C	O	S.S.E R	BH	B·V BU		T·L
MAY F 23	219	219	212	217						
S 24	218	218	217	218	1⁴		0	0 1⁴		4 T
M 26	219	219	217	217		2		¼		
T 27	218	219	217	219						2 T
W 28	220	226	220	225	0		7	0	1	
T 29	226	226	221	221		6				
S 31	219	220	217	217				0 8		¼
JUN M 2	218	219	214	214	6²		0	3²		7⁴
T 3	216	219	215	217		5				
W 4	218	219	216	216		¼				5 T
T 5	217	217	216	217	3²		0	½	1	
F 6	217	218	216	217		2⁴				
S 7	217	218	216	216				9⁴ 7⁴	2²	
M 9	216	214	213	214	4⁵		1²	2¹		
T 10	214	214	213	213		³⁄₈		⁷⁄₈		
W 11	212	212	210	210				−¹⁰	1²	
T 12	210	212	209	209	3²		½ 1²			
F 13	204	206	205	205		½		4		
S 14	205	207	204	205				7⁵ ⅞	1⁴	
M 16	205	206	204	205	3		0	0		
T 17	206	206	206	206		5¹				
W 18	208	211	208	210		1³		4⁵	6⁴ T	
T 19	211	211	210	211	1		³⁄₄ 0	+⁵		
F 20	210	210	207	208		³⁄₄		2²		
S 21	204	211	204	211		¼		4 5⁷	1 T	
M 23	211	212	204	211	1⁶		1 ¼			
T 24	210	211	209	209		1⁶		−⁴	1²	
W 25	208	210	205	210						
T 26	210	210	209	209	1⁴		¼ 0	−²		
F 27	209	209	208	208		¼		1		
S 28	208	209	207	208				3² 2	0	
M 30	209	212	209	212	0		7⁴ 3⁶	0		
JUL T 1	213	216	213	216		7⁴		+7		
W 2	216	216	214	214					7² T	
T 3	214	214	213	213	3²		0 1²			

Right table — WK

	O	H	L	C	O	S.S.E R	BH	B·V BU		T·L
S 5	213	217	213	215		4⁴		3² 12		
M 7	217	217	215	216		¼				4⁴ T
T 8	216	219	216	219	1⁶	4⁶ 1⁴	0			
W 9	219	221	219	219		2²		+12²		
T 10	220	222	220	222						7 T
F 11	223	232	222	230	½	7¹ 9¹	0			
S 12	230	230	228	228				2 12⁴		
M 14	227	230	227	227	3⁶					7⁴
T 15	227	232	226	230		9²·¹ 1⁶	½			
W 16	231	235	231	233				+2⁴		5⁶
T 17	231	232	228	228	6²					
F 18	226	230	226	230		5²·¹	0 2			
S 19	226	231	226	230				10 14⁴		
M 21	231	232	228	230		2				7² T
T 22	232	232	229	231	3⁴	3²·¹	0 0			
W 23	230	233	230	231				−3		
T 24	231	231	226	229						1⁶
F 25	229	229	226	227	5	3¹	0 2⁴			
S 26	226	226	226	227				8⁴ 6²		
M 28	226	227	225	225						1²
T 29	222	222	215	216	2⁴	6²·⁴	0 9⁶			
W 30	218	221	218	221		4⁶		−3⁶		
T 31	232	226	224	225			1² 0			10 T
AUG F 1	226	227	225	225	1	1		3⁴ 7²		
S 2	223	226	223	223		4				5 T
M 4	225	230	225	227	5	2²·¹	0 ¼			
T 5	227	232	225	225				+7⁴		
W 6	225	227	224	224						1
T 7	224	226	226	225	0	3²	0			
F 8	226	229	226	227		7¹		5 10⁴		
S 9	229	234	229	231						7
M 11	231	233	226	227	6	1⁶	0 0			
T 12	230	231	227	227		1²		+¹		
W 13	227	228	226	227		1²				3 T
T 14	225	230	228	229						

FIGURE 19

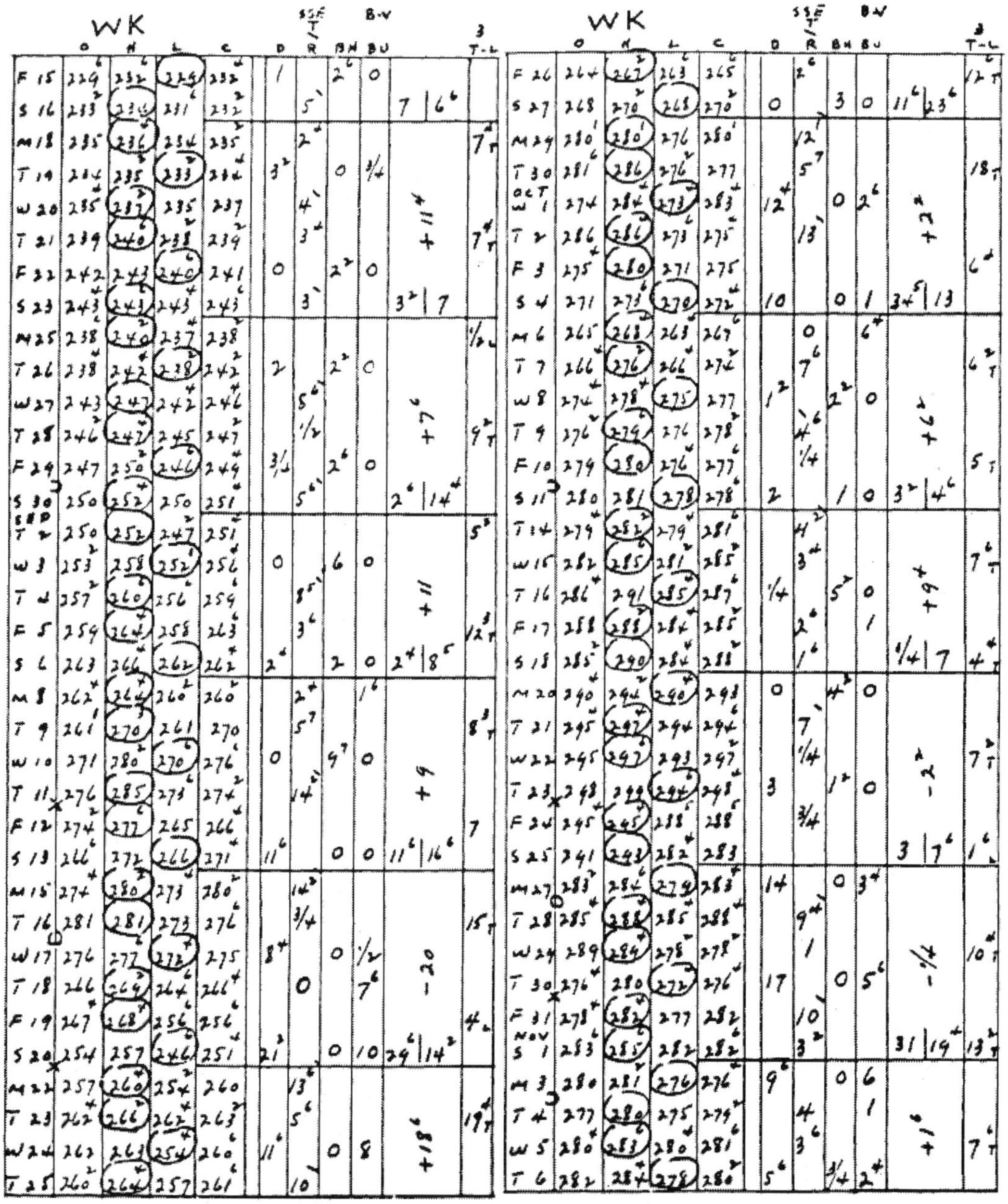

WK

	O	H	L	C	D	SSE T R	B-V BH	BU		3 T-L
F 15	229^6	232^6	229	232^4	1		2^6	0		
S 16	233^2	234	231^6	232^2		5			$7 \mid 6^6$	
M 18	235	236^4	234	235^2		2^4				7^2 T
T 19	234	235^3	233^2	234^4	3^2		0	3/4		
W 20	235	237^2	235	237		4			$+11^4$	
T 21	239	240^6	238^2	239^2		3^4				7^4 T
F 22	242	243	240^6	241	0		2^2	0		
S 23	243^4	243^6	243^4	243^6		3			$3^2 \mid 7$	
M 25	238^6	240^2	237^4	238^2						1/2 L
T 26	238^4	242^4	238^2	242^2	2		2^2	0		
W 27	243	247	242^4	246^4		5^6				
T 28	246^2	247^4	245	247^2		1/2			$+7^6$	9^2 T
F 29	247	250^2	246^6	249^4	3/4		2^6	0		
S 30	250	252^4	250	251^4		5^6			$2^6 \mid 14^4$	
SEP T 2	250	252	247^2	251^2						5^3
W 3	253^2	258	252^1	256^4	0		6	0		
T 4	257^2	260^6	256^2	259^6		8^5			+11	
F 5	259	264^4	258	263^6		3^6				12^3 T
S 6	263	266^4	262	262^4	2^4		2	0	$2^4 \mid 8^5$	
M 8	262^4	264^4	260^2	260^2		2^4		1^6		
T 9	261^1	270^3	261	270		5^7				8^3 T
W 10	271	280^2	270^6	276^6	0		9^7	0		
T 11	276	285	273^6	274^2		14^2			+9	
F 12	274^2	277^6	265	266^4						7
S 13	266^6	272	266	271^4	11^6		0	0	$11^6 \mid 16^6$	
M 15	274^4	280^3	273^4	280^2		14^3				
T 16	281	281	273	276^6		3/4				15 T
W 17	276	277^2	272^4	275	8^4		0	1/2	−20	
T 18	266	264^3	264^6	266^4		0		7^6		
F 19	267^4	268^4	256^6	256^6						4 L
S 20	254	257	246^6	251^4	21^3		0	10	$29^6 \mid 14^2$	
M 22	257	260^4	254^2	260		13^6				
T 23	262^4	266^2	262^4	263^2		5^6				19^4 T
W 24	262	263	254^4	260^6	11^6		0	8	$+18^6$	
T 25	260^2	264^4	257	261^6		10				

WK

	O	H	L	C	D	SSE T R	B-V BH	BU		3 T-L
F 26	264	267^2	263^6	265^6		2^6				12^6 T
S 27	268	270^2	268	270^2	0		3	0	$11^6 \mid 23^6$	
M 29	280^1	280^1	276	280^1		12^1				
T 30	281^6	286	276^2	277		5^7				18 T
OCT W 1	274	284^4	273^4	283^4	12^4		0	2^6	$+7^4$	
T 2	286	286^2	273^6	275^4		13				
F 3	275^4	280	271	275						6^4
S 4	271	273^6	270	272^4	10		0	1	$34^5 \mid 13$	
M 6	265	268^2	263^4	267^6		0		6^4		
T 7	266^4	276^2	266^4	274^2		7^6				6^2 T
W 8	274^4	278^4	275	277	1^2		2^2	0	$+7^2$	
T 9	276^2	279^6	276	278^2		4^6				
F 10	279	280	276^4	277^6		1/4				5 T
S 11	280	281	278	278^6	2		1	0	$3^2 \mid 4^6$	
T 14	279^4	282^2	279^4	281^6		4^2				
W 15	282	285^6	281^2	285^2		3^4				7^6 T
T 16	286^4	291	285^4	287^6	1/4		5^2	0	$+9^4$	
F 17	288	288^2	284^4	285^2		2^6		1		
S 18	285^2	290	284^4	288^2		1^6			$1/4 \mid 7$	4^4 T
M 20	290^4	294^2	290^4	293	0		4^2	0		
T 21	295^4	297^4	294	294^6		7				
W 22	295	297^6	293	297^2		1/4			-2^2	7^2 T
T 23	298	299	294^6	298^4	3		1^2	0		
F 24	295^4	295^4	288^6	288^6		3/4				
S 25	291	293	282^4	283					$3 \mid 7^6$	1^6 L
M 27	283^2	284^6	279	283^4	14		0	3^4		
T 28	285^4	288^2	285^4	288^4		9^4				
W 29	289	289^4	278^4	278^2		1			−1/4	10^4 T
T 30	276^4	280	272^2	276^4	17		0	5^6		
F 31	278^4	282^2	277	282		10				
NOV S 1	283^6	285^2	282	282^6		3^2			$31 \mid 19^4$	13^2 T
M 3	280	281^2	276	276^4	9^6		0	6		
T 4	277	280	275	279^2		4		1	$+1^6$	
W 5	280^4	283^6	280^4	281^6		3^6				7^6 T
T 6	282	284^4	278	280^2	5^6		3/4	2^4		

FIGURE 20

FIGURE 21

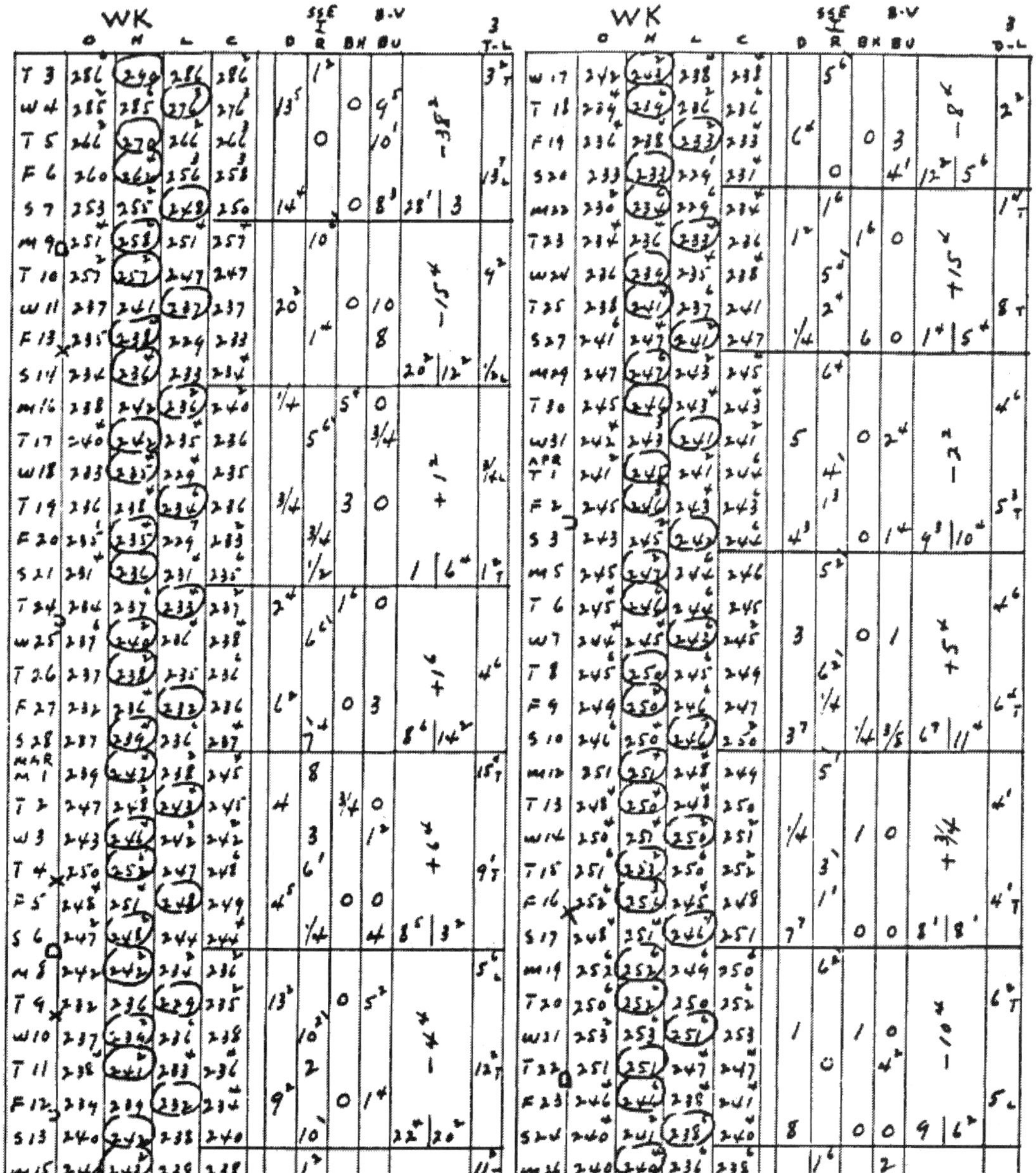

This handwritten trading ledger (Figure 22) records daily price and session data in two side-by-side blocks.

	O	H	L	C	D	SSE R	BK	BU		3 T-L
T 3	286	290	286	286		1²				3⁷
W 4	285	285	276	276	13⁵		0	9⁵		
T 5	266	270	266	266		0		10¹	-38⁴	
F 6	260	262	256	258	14⁴					13²
S 7	253	255	248	250		0	8³	28¹	3	
M 9	251	253	251	257	10					
T 10	257	257	247	247					-15⁴	4²
W 11	247	241	232	237	20³		0	10		
F 13	235	238	229	233		1⁴		8		
S 14	234	236	233	234					20²|12²	½₆
M 16	238	242	236	240	½⁴	5⁴	0			
T 17	240	242	235	236		5⁶		¾		
W 18	233	233	229	235					+	½₆
T 19	236	238	234	236	¾		3	0	+	
F 20	235	235	229	233		¾				
S 21	231	236	231	235		½			1|6⁴	1⁷ T
T 24	234	237	233	237	2⁴	1⁶	0			
W 25	237	240	236	238		6⁶			+⁶	4⁶
T 26	237	238	235	236					+	
F 27	232	236	232	236	6⁵		0	3		6⁴ T
S 28	237	239	236	237	7³				8⁶|14²	
MAR M 1	239	242	238	245	8					15⁷ T
T 2	247	248	242	245	4	¾	0		+⁶	
W 3	243	246	242	242		3		1²	+	
T 4	250	253	247	248	6¹					9⁷ T
F 5	248	251	248	249	4⁵		0	0	+	
S 6	247	248	244	244		¼		4	8⁶|3²	
M 8	242	242	234	236						5⁶ ₆
T 9	232	236	229	235	13⁵		0	5²	+⁴	
W 10	237	234	236	238	10²					
T 11	238	241	233	236	2		0	1⁴	-	12⁷ T
F 12	234	234	232	234	9²					
S 13	240	242	238	240	10		0		22⁴|20²	
M 15	240	241	238	238	1²					11⁷ T
T 16	239	241	237	241	5⁶		0	½		

	O	H	L	C	D	SSE R	BK	BU		3 D-L
W 17	242	242	238	238		5⁶			+⁶	
T 18	234	239	236	236					-	2²
F 19	236	238	233	233	6⁴		0	3		
S 20	233	233	224	231		0	4¹	12²|5⁶		
M 22	230	234	229	234		1⁶				1⁷ T
T 23	234	236	233	236	1²		1⁶	0	+⁵|4	
W 24	236	234	235	238		5⁶			+⁵|4	
T 25	238	241	237	241		2⁴		6	0	8 T
S 27	241	247	241	247	¼		6	0	1⁴|5⁶	
M 29	247	247	243	245		6⁴				
T 30	245	246	243	243						4⁶
W 31	242	243	241	241	5		0	2⁴	-²	
APR T 1	241	246	241	244		4¹			-	
F 2	245	246	243	243		1³				5³ T
S 3	243	245	242	244	4³		0	1⁴	4³|10⁴	
M 5	245	247	244	246		5²				
T 6	245	246	244	245					+⁵	4⁶
W 7	244	245	243	245	3		0	1	+⁵	
T 8	245	250	245	249		6²				6⁴ T
F 9	249	250	246	247		¼				6⁴ T
S 10	246	250	246	250	3⁷		¼|3/8	6⁷|11⁴		
M 12	251	251	248	249		5¹				
T 13	248	250	248	250						4⁴
W 14	250	251	250	251	¼		1	0	¾|4	
T 15	251	252	250	252		3¹			+	
F 16	252	254	245	248		1¹				4⁵ T
S 17	248	251	246	251	7²		0	0	8¹|8¹	
M 19	252	252	249	250		6²				
T 20	250	251	250	252					+|4	6⁷ T
W 21	253	253	251	253	1		1	0	-|4	
T 22	251	251	247	247		0	4²	-		
F 23	246	246	238	241						5⁶ ₆
S 24	240	241	238	240	8		0	0	9|6²	
M 26	240	240	236	235	1⁶		2			
T 27	234	242	239	240	2					3⁴ T

FIGURE 22

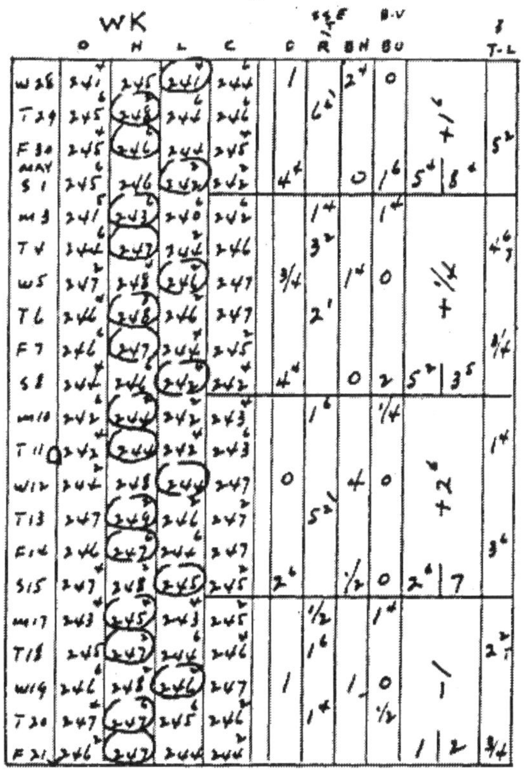

SUMMARY

Closing Prices May 23, 1947 .... 217¾
Closing Prices May 21, 1948 .... 244¼

Long Pull Position (Gain Pts.) 26½
Decline and Rally Column Pts.
Total Fluctuations 912⅞

DAILY TRADING
Approximately 35 times the Long Pull Position

BOOK TRADING
No. of Declines (Buying Days) 100
" " Rallies (Selling Days) 100
Decline Pts. (Short Sales) 456
Rally Pts. (Long Sales) 456⅞
No. of times Sale Day sold thru (BH)
  Long Sales 55
" " " SSE exceeded (Sale Day High)
    Short Sales 50
" " " BH exceeded (Short Sale) 49

" " " BU Buy Day Low under
    (Short Sale Low) 49
" " BV Buy Day Low was Violated 34
  Three (3) Day Swing Method
Number of 3 day swings 100
  " " Gain Day Swings 89
  " " Gain Day Swings that sold thru
    'T' on Sale Day 54
  " " Loss Day Swings 11
  " " Gain Day Points 524½
  " " Loss Day Points 21
  " " Short Sale Points 456

Net Total Long Points 503½
Short Sale Points 456

Total Long and Short Pts. 959½

No summary is made of the short sale points made
from the short sale on Buying Day High made First

FIGURE 23

Figure 24

1947	CK '48' O	H	L	C	S&E O	R	BH	BU	3 T·L
MAY F 23	143³	144²	142	143		4²		2⁶ 8¹	
S 24	144	144	142	143	2²		0	3/4	1
M 26	144	145	143	143		3⁹			7⁷
T 27	144	146¹	143²	146		1³			+⁷₇
W 28	144	151	148	152	0		8	0	
T 29	152	152	150	151¹		3⁶			
S 31	150	150	149	149				2³ 7² 1⁶	
JUN M 2	153	153	150	151	0		3	0	
T 3	154	156	153	155		6³			7⁷₇
W 4	156	158	155	156		1⁵			
T 5	157	157	155	155	3³		0	1/4	
F 6	157	157	155	156		2⁶			
S 7	157	157	154	154				3³ 9 2⁶₇	
M 9	154	155	153	155	4²		0	1	
T 10	155	157	153	156		3⁴			
W 11	156	157	155	156		3/4			4²₇
T 12	158	160	153	154	4²		2²	2	
F 13	154	155	151	152		2²		2²	
S 14	153	154	152	153				8⁴ 5⁶ 3/4	
M 16	151	151	149	149	5²		0	3	
T 17	150	152	150	151		4¹			
W 18	151	156	153	156		3⁴			7⁴₇
T 19	157	159	156	158	0		2⁶	0	
F 20	156	158	154	155		1⁴		1⁶	
S 21	157	157	155	156				5² 5⁴ 3⁴	
M 23	156	155	156	155	1		1⁴	0	
T 24	154	160	158	158		4⁴			5 ₇
W 25	158	161	157	160		1/2			
T 26	161	162	159	160	1⁶		1³	0	
F 27	160	161	158	154		1⁴		3/4	
S 28	158	159	157	157				2⁶ 6 1 ₗ	
M 30	157	160	157	160	7,8	2²	0		
T JUL 1	160	161	159	159		3³			3
W 2	159	160	155	154	1⁷		0	0	
T 3	154	163	158	159					

	CK O	H	L	C	SSE O	R	BH	BU	3 T·L
S 5	161	163	160	163²		4²		2⁶ 8¹	
M 7	163	166	163	166	2⁶				7⁷
T 8	164	166	164	165⁷	2²		0	0	
W 9	166	172	166	171		8²¹			
T 10	172	172	172	174		4⁶			13⁷
F 11	176	181	173	178	4		4	0	
S 12	178	180	176	178		7		6³ 15²	
M 14	177	181	172	181		1⁷			8⁷₇
T 15	181	184	179	183	2¹	4⁶ 2³	0		
W 16	181	184	174	181				·/4	1
T 17	179	179	175	175				+	1/4
F 18	174	177	173	176	5⁶		0	1²	
S 19	176	179	176	174		6¹		7⁷ 10⁷	
M 21	181	184	178	181		4¹			10⁷₇
T 22	183	184	181	182	3		0	0	
W 23	182	185	182	183		4⁵			4⁴₇
T 24	183	184	180	182					3
F 25	181	182	180	180	4		0	3/4	
S 26	179	184	179	183		4³		7 8⁷	
M 28	183	184	181	181		5/3			4⁷₇
T 29	186	187	176	178	8⁵		0	5²	
W 30	180	182	180	181		6¹			13⁴₇
T 31	183	189	183	189		7⁴			
AUG F 1	191	193	189	190	1/4		3⁶	0	
S 2	191	195	190	193		6¹		8⁷ 12	
M 4	149	201	196	201		5⁷			11⁷₇
T 5	198	201	196	198	4⁷		0	0	
W 6	199	203	197	197		6¹			3²
T 7	198	199	195	199					
F 8	202	206	203	206	0	2³	7¹	0	
S 9	209	214	208	214		12³		4⁷ 14¹	
M 11	213	218	206	208		4			16³₇
T 12	212	213	205	216	12⁵		0	5/8	
W 13	205	205	201	202		5/8		4⁶	
T 14	204	207	204	207		1³			2 ₇

This is a handwritten trading/price chart ledger. The two halves are transcribed as tables. Headers across the top read: CK | O H L C | SEF | D·V | 3. Sub-headers: O | H | L | C | D | R | BH | BU | T·L

Date	O	H	L	C	D	R	BH	BU			T·L
F 15	205	214	208	213	0		7	0			
S 16	215	215	208	210		7			12⁵	7⁵	
M 18	218	218	215	216		3¹					10
T 19	214	214	210	212	7		0	4⁴			
W 20	215	217	214	216		6⁴			+16		
T 21	215	222	215	220		5²					11
F 22	224	226	222	222	0		4⁴	0			
S 23	223	226	220	226		4⁴		16	7⁹	11	
M 25	214	221	218	218							½
T 26	218	220	214	219	7²		0	4¹			
W 27	220	221	218	220		7¹			+6		
T 28	214	220	217	218					—1		6
F 29	217	220	217	220	3²		0	½			
S 30	221	222	221	221		5²			10⁴	:12	
SEP T 2	220	223	214	223		¾					6
W 3	224	228	224	227	0		4⁶	0	+5⁴		
T 4	227	228	225	226		4¹					
F 5	225	228	224	228							3
S 6	227	229	225	227	2⁴		1⁴	0	2⁴	4	
M 8	226	226	225	227		3²		½			
T 9	228	235	228	235		6⁵			+6²		9
W 10	237	242	235	240	0		7⁵	0			
T 11	241	244	235	235		8⁴		¾	+4		
F 12	235	237	227	230							1
S 13	229	237	226	233	7⁶		0	0	7⁶	11⁶	
M 15	235	240	234	240		10⁶					
T 16	239	244	233	238					—21⁸		10
W 17	238	238	234	236	5²		0	0			
T 18	230	232	228	228		0		6¹	—1		
F 19	227	234	220	220							44
S 20	213	214	212	212	17⁵		0	8	22⁷	10⁶	
M 22	215	221	212	215		8¹			+8⁶		6
T 23	217	218	210	212							
W 24	212	212	208	212	11⁸		0	3⁵	+4		
T 25	213	217	210	214		10¹					

Right table

Date	O	H	L	C	D	R	BH	BU			T·L
F 26	216	218	215	216		1²					11
S 27	218	221	218	220	¼		2⁶	0	11⁵	18¹	
M 29	224	228	224	228		10⁷					
T 30	233	234	226	226		5⁵					16
OCT W 1	225	232	224	232	10²		0	2	—3		
T 2	233	233	224	224		4³					
F 3	224	232	218	221							26
S 4	218	219	216	217	10⁶		0	2⁴	21	20¹	
M 6	213	217	210	217		1²	5⁶				
T 7	218	221	216	219		3⁶			+3		5
W 8	220	223	219	220	1⁴		2⁴	0	+4		
T 9	219	221	218	219		2		1			
F 10	219	219	215	217		1²			1⁴		0
S 11	221	223	220	221	0		4	0	1⁴	3²	
T 14	223	224	221	223		3⁷			+4		6
W 15	223	226	221	226		2²					
T 16	226	229	226	227	½		3	0	+4		
F 17	227	227	224	224		1²		1⁴			
S 18	224	224	222	224					½	5¹	1²
M 20	227	228	222	228	0		4	0			
T 21	229	230	227	228		4²¹			—¼		1²
W 22	227	227	225	226		0		3⁴			
T 23	225	226	222	222	5²		0	5⁵			
F 24	221	222	216	216		0			5²	4²	3⁴
S 25	218	219	212	215							
M 27	215	216	213	215	5²		0	0			
T 28	215	216	215	214		5⁶			+7		7
W 29	214	220	212	214		1⁴					
T 30	214	216	211	216	4		0	½	+4		
F 31	217	221	216	221		4⁴					
NOV S 1	232	223	220	221		2			14²	15²	11
M 3	220	222	219	221	4		0	1			
T 4	221	222	220	223		4⁴			+7		
W 5	224	226	224	226	3						7
T 6	226	227	223	225	3⁴		3½	3½	+4		7

FIGURE 25

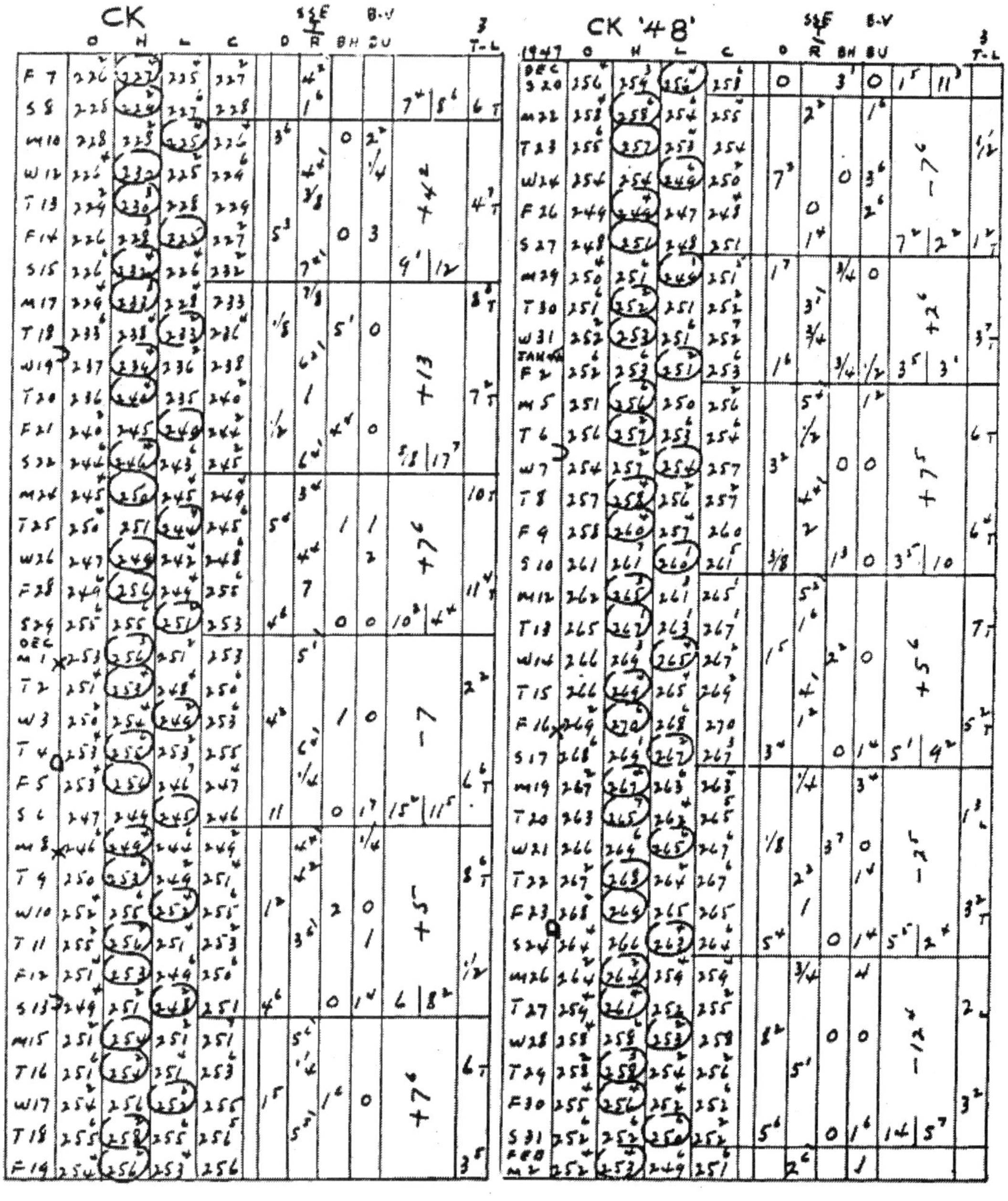

FIGURE 26

	CK					SSE I		B.V		3
	O	H	L	C	D	R	BH	BU		T-L
T 3	251	252	247	247						1⁶
W 4	246	247	233	234	12⁷		0	7⁷	-36⁶	
T 5	233	233	231	231		0		8		
F 6	223	226	223	223						13⁵
S 7	217	217	215	215	10⁵		0	8	23⁴ 2⁶	
M 9	215	223	211	221		8		4⁶		
T 10	220	220	213	213					-19⁴	4⁸
W 11	205	205	205	305	14⁶		0	8		
F 13	197	204	197	197		0		8		
S 14	200	202	192	196					14⁶ 5	1⁶
M 16	200	204	198	204	5²		1'	0		
T 17	205	204	205	206		11'				3⁸
W 18	205	210	205	210		3/4			+15·⁴	11⁴
T 19	211	213	206	211	3/4		3	0		
F 20	211	212	207	209	2⁶					
S 21	209	212	208	211					6 13⁶	2⁶
T 24	211	216	210	216	1⁶		4⁴	0		
W 25	216	216	216	218		4²			+8²	
T 26	218	218	215	217						8²
F 27	215	216	213	216	4⁶		0	1⁴		
S 28	217	223	216	220		7²			6⁴ 16⁴	
MAR M 1	221	228	221	227			13	0		14⁷
T 2	227	229	224	226	3⁵				+4⁴	
W 3	226	229	223	226		5		3/4		
T 4	224	231	228	228		1⁶				6⁴
F 5	224	230	228	228	3²		0	0		
S 6	228	228	224	224		1/2		4	6² 5⁴	
M 8	222	223	216	216						5⁶
T 9	210	214	208	213	14³		0	7⁵		
W 10	215	217	214	216		4'			+4²	
T 11	216	218	209	212		1²				10⁸
F 12	213	213	207	210	11⁴		0	1⁴		
S 13	215	218	214	218		11³			25⁶ 2⁶	
M 15	218	223	212	214		4³				15⁷
T 16	214	221	218	220	5		0	0		

	CK					SSE I		B.V		3
	O	H	L	C	D	R	BH	BU		T-L
W 17	221	220	218	218		6				1
T 18	218	218	213	216					-6⁴	
F 19	215	216	213	213	6²		0	3/4		
S 20	214	214	206	211		1⁷		3'	11² 7⁷	
M 22	211	216	210	215		1³				3⁴ T
T 23	215	216	213	216	2²		1/2	0	+8²	
W 24	215	217	215	216		3⁴				2⁶
T 25	216	216	214	216						
S 27	216	220	216	219	0		3⁶	0	2³ 3⁴	
M 29	220	220	218	220		4³				3⁶
T 30	219	220	218	218						3⁶
W 31	216	217	215	215	5'		0	2⁷	1/4	
APR T 1	215	221	215	221		6⁸			1	
F 2	221	223	215	218		3/4				7⁴ T
S 3	217	219	216	216	5⁴		0	1⁴	10⁵ 10⁶	
M 5	220	221	218	220		4⁴				3⁴
T 6	220	221	218	218						3³
W 7	218	221	217	220	3³		1/8	3/4	+5⁴	
T 8	221	226	221	226		8⁶				
F 9	226	228	225	225		2				10⁶ T
S 10	225	226	223	224	3⁴		1	0	6⁷ 13⁷	
M 12	229	229	226	226		4⁶				
T 13	226	229	226	228						4
W 14	229	230	228	230	1/4		1⁴	0	2	
T 15	230	234	230	233		5²			1	
F 16	233	234	224	225		1/2				5⁶ T
S 17	225	227	223	227	11		0	1⁷	11⁶ 10	
M 19	229	226	222	224		6²		1		
T 20	224	225	221	223						2²
W 21	224	227	222	226	3		0	0	10²	
T 22	224	224	221	221		2⁴		1		
F 23	221	224	215	216	6²		0	1/2	9² 8⁶	1² T
S 24	215	219	214	216						
M 26	215	215	212	215		1/4		2'		
T 27	216	219	216	217		4				4² T

FIGURE 27

85

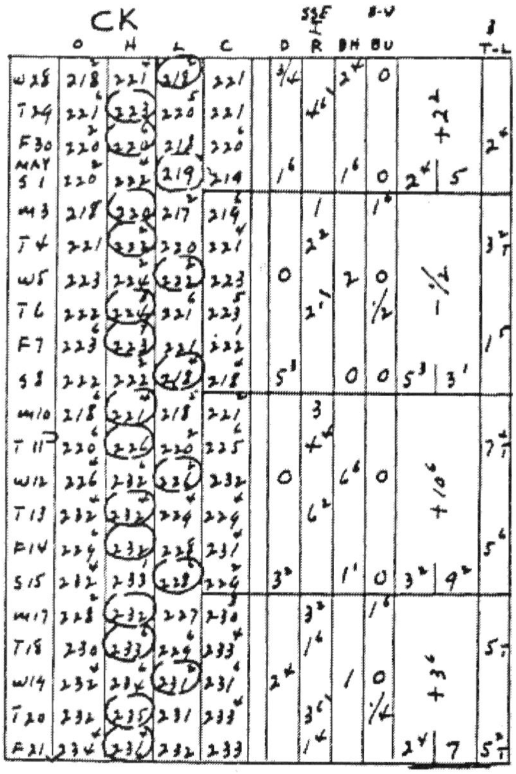

SUMMARY

Closing Prices May 23, 1947 143
Closing Prices May 21, 1948 233

Long Pull Position (Gain) Pts. 90
Decline and Rally Column Pts.
Total Fluctuations 898⅝

DAILY TRADING
Approximately 10 times the Long Pull Position

BOOK TRADING
No. of Declines (Buying Days) 100
No. of Rallies (Selling Days) 100
Decline Pts. (Short Sales) 416⅝
Rally Points (Long Sales) 482
No. of times Sale Day sold thru (BH)
    Long Sales 66
  " " " SSE exceeded (Sale Day High)
    Short Sales 53
    " " BH exceeded (Short Sale) 50

" " " Buy Day low under
    (Short Sale Low) 42
" " " BV Buy Day Low was Violated... 39
Three (3) Day Swing Method
Number of 3 day swings 100
  " " Gain day swings 88
  " " Gain day swings that sold thru
    'T' on Sale Day 57
  " " Loss day swings 12
  " " Gain day points 567
  " " Loss day points 36¼
  " " Short Sale points 416⅝

Net Total Long Points 530¾
Short Sale Points 416⅝

Total Long and Short Points 947⅞

No summary is made of the short sale points made
from the short sale on Buying Day High made First

FIGURE 28

Portfolio

Revised Reprint from

Taylor Trading Techniique For Trading in Stocks

This illustration is from a trading-book started after an 8 point decline in the RR: Averages—DI, and worked forward from the low of the stock (51 3/8); the lowest point reached during the first 10 days of trading.

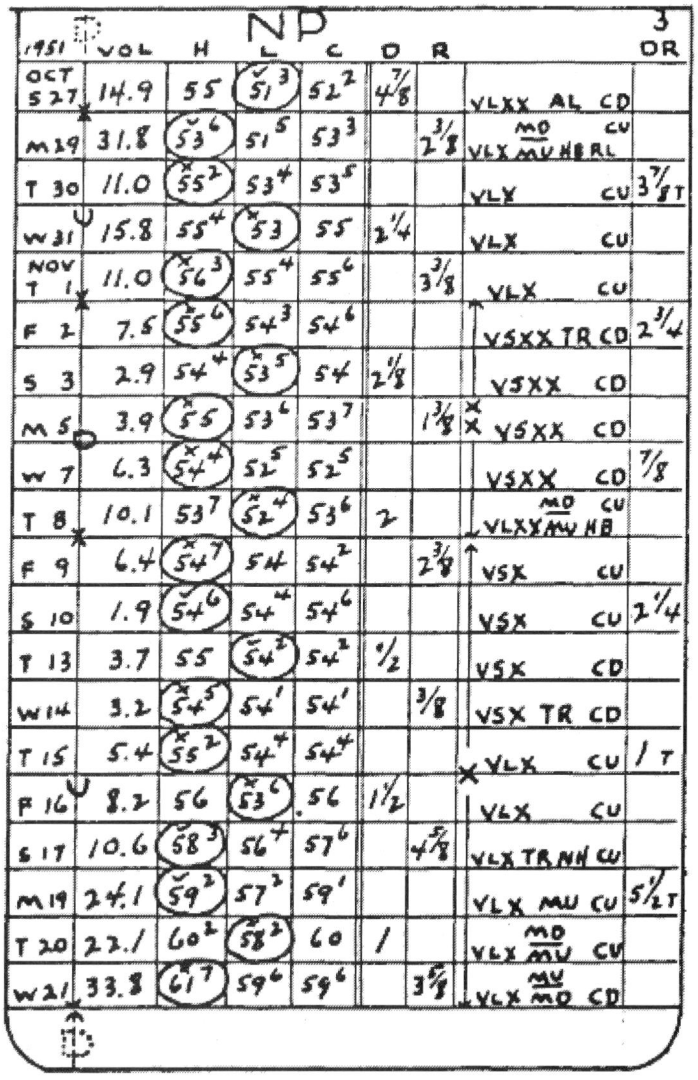

1951	VOL	H	L	C	D	R	NP	3 OR
OCT S 27	14.9	55	51^{3}	52^{2}	4 7/8		VLXX AL CD	
M 29	31.8	53^{6}	51^{5}	53^{3}		2 3/8	VLX MD/MU HB RL CU	
T 30	11.0	55^{2}	53^{4}	53^{5}			VLX CU	3 7/8 T
W 31	15.8	55^{4}	53	55	2 1/4		VLX CU	
NOV T 1	11.0	56^{3}	55^{4}	55^{6}		3 3/8	VLX CU	
F 2	7.5	55^{6}	54^{3}	54^{6}			VSXX TR CD	2 3/4
S 3	2.9	54^{4}	53^{5}	54	2 1/8		VSXX CD	
M 5	3.9	55	53^{6}	53^{7}		1 3/8	X X VSXX CD	
W 7	6.3	54^{4}	52^{5}	52^{5}			VSXX CD	7/8
T 8	10.1	53^{7}	52^{4}	53^{6}	2		VLXX MD/MU HB CU	
F 9	6.4	54^{7}	54	54^{2}		2 3/8	VSX CU	
S 10	1.9	54^{6}	54^{4}	54^{6}			VSX CU	2 1/4
T 13	3.7	55	54^{2}	54^{2}	1/2		VSX CD	
W 14	3.2	54^{5}	54^{1}	54^{1}		3/8	VSX TR CD	
T 15	5.4	55^{2}	54^{4}	54^{4}			X VLX CU	1 T
F 16	8.2	56	53^{6}	56	1 1/2		VLX CU	
S 17	10.6	58^{3}	56^{7}	57^{6}		4 5/8	VLX TR NH CU	
M 19	24.1	59^{2}	57^{2}	59^{1}			VLX MU CU	5 1/2 T
T 20	22.1	60^{2}	58^{2}	60	1		VLX MD/MU CU	
W 21	33.8	61^{7}	59^{6}	59^{6}		3 5/8	VLX MU/MD CD	

Figure 29

Abbreviations used in trading

CD - closed down on day or previous close
CU - closed up on day or previous close
NH - new high, since last trend high
NL - new low, since last trend low
HB - higher (support) bottom, or last trend low
MU - mark-up, big support buying (comparative)
MD - mark-down, big selling (comparative)
RH - real high, on greater or less volume
AH - actual high, on greater or less volume
RL - real low, on greater or less volume
AL - actual low, on greater or less volume
TR - trend reversal (supplementary rule)
X - up-trading area
XX - down-trading area
V - volume; represents all factors combined; movement; price changes; news, etc., modified as large VL, or small VS (used compartively to previous daily volume)
VLX - increasing on rally
VSX - decreasing on rally
VLXX - increasing on decline
VSXX - decreasing on decline

Used daily the symbols form an important concise record of the movement. At places of abnormal increased volume, important—trend change may be near. MU/MD shows big buying, immediately reversed at high into big selling, as shown by closing price of day. MU first big selling, then big buying, as shown as close.

PLACE THIS SHEET ALONGSIDE PAGES FOR READY REFERENCE.

The records of the past, for many years, show the market to have a definite 1-2-3 rhythm, varied at times with an extra beat of 1-2-3-4 and at times 5. These figures represent days. The market goes up 1-2-3 days, then reacts; the 4th and 5th figure is the variation when it runs that extra day or two on the way up or down, in both bull and bear trends. This 1-2-3 beat of the market [is] subject to these occasional variations (usually caused by internal market conditions and news announcements—also, at the climax of extended trends up or down) occur with surprising regularity. So it would seem that the same methods of manipulation used in the past—in start-big and continuing a trend—are still used today. That is buying and then selling, every third or fourth day in an up-trend and reversed in a downtrend. Three days are considered as a trading cycle for active traders; who will be guided by the action around their buying and selling objectives. Those who are using the longer term trends will take their cue from the signs present at the trend change points—explained in the latter pages. Can be recorded in an ordinary 5 3/4" x 3 3/4"," ruled note book by drawing the perpendicular lines to form the columns. The example, opposite page, is a record of the actual trading in this stock. Observe the markings!

TO MAKE-UP TRADING BOOK:

First head-line it with the year, above first column, then in the first column put in the month, starting day and date.

The next four columns are for Volume, High, Low, and Closing Prices.

These entries are recorded daily for a period of Ten (10) Days; then the lowest price reached during this period is ringed, and termed a Buying Day.

Working backward or forward from this low; the two ringed prices under the "F" are termed 1st and 2nd Selling days. The 1st follows a Buying Day, and the 2nd precedes it.

A trading book started from any date should always be made-up in the above manner, so 'that it reads: A Buying Day, 1st Selling Day, 2nd Selling Day, then a Buying Day, 1st Selling Day, 2nd Selling Day; then a buying Day, etc.

The book is always kept in this same order; **never change the continuity from the way it was started**. No lines are left open for 'Sundays or Holidays; the market is considered a series of continuous trading sessions, without a break.

THE (D) COLUMN—DECLINE COLUMN

This column shows the unit of decline from the high of previous day (2nd Selling Day) to low of Buying Day. (See Oct. 27-3 1, etc.).

When no decline occurs; put in a Zero.

The zero does not occur often, but when it does it shows higher support above the low of previous day, and it generally means nearby higher prices, for a day, and at times longer. (See Dec. 5, Feb. 8).

When the decline unit is large; the rally unit is generally small. (See Oct. 27-29, Dec. 8-10, Feb. 5-6).

THE (R) COLUMN—RALLY COLUMN

This column shows the extent of the rally from low of Buying to the high of 1st Selling Day, and the amount of decline in "D" column, recovered. (See Oct. 29, Nov. 1, etc.).

When no rally occurs; put in a Zero.

The zero does not occur often, but when it does it shows lower support, under the low of previous day, and it generally means nearby lower prices, for a day, and at times longer.

When the decline unit is small; the rally unit is generally large. (See Nov. 16-17, Dec. 16-17, Dec. 5-6, Mar. 27-28).

(The "D" and "H" columns are used by the tape-reading traders. Using the low of Buying Day and high of 1st Selling Day, as their buying and selling objectives.)

THE (3 D R) COLUMN—THREE DAY RALLY COLUMN

This column shows the extent of the rally from low of Buying Day to high of 2nd Selling day.

When the swing shows a loss; put in the loss unit with the "L" beside it. (See Jan. 31, April 2). When the rally shows a gain; put in the gain unit only. When the rally shows a gain, exceeding the high of 1ˢᵗ Selling Day, put in the gain unit and the "T" alongside—meaning "sold through" the high or previous day. These are strong rallies, in most cases, but when the unit is comparatively large, it shows a comparative big interest and volume in the stock; and many times it occurs, at, or prior to the start or reversal or an uptrend. (Nov. 27, Feb. 7, March 29).

The Trend Line of the stock is drawn alongside the Date column. Use a Blue line for an uptrend and Red for downtrend. This line points out the actual highs and lows of Trading Areas. Between the arrow-heads "U" means up, "D" down.

The action around tops and bottoms of trading areas, intermediate and primary swings are explained in the latter pages; the following is a supplementary rule to this action, and can generally be seen near the trend change points, usually the day after high or low: has been made:So long as the price on the rally continues to make a new high, with the price on the reaction holding above the last low, with the price on the next rally going higher than the last high—the trend is UP. Failure of the price on the rally to make a new high, with the price on the reaction going lower than the last low—would reverse the trend to Down (See Nov. 2-14-17-23, Dec. 3-7, Feb. 4-11, Mar. 27-31).

All extended trends are interrupted by trading declines and rallies, and they, also, show this "rule" action at the reversals—a trader expects them, but does not try to capitalize all of them, not if he is trading the longer swings. He knows they are of a temporary nature, if in the early stages of the main movement. These minor movements [show] the same general characteristics and pattern, but they, also, have a distinguishing action. They show in a less pronounced degree; increased volume, at the tops and bottoms, compared to the previous daily trading.

The salient features of important tops and bottoms; big market participation; interest in the stock; fast mark-ups, or down; big intersection price changes (see units in the 2 day column),

and volume—are lacking.

These factors are noticeably absent after the minor trend changes and as the decline continues, and at the low, the volume may or may not increase before the trend again changes, but generally it does. After the trend changes the volume shows a progressive increase as the rise is resumed—when the major movement is to be continued. During these corrective periods the trend is contained between the last important high and low, and can go either way, up or down, but in the early stages of the major movement it can be assumed as, up. The price of necessity fails to make new highs with the lows going lower during this period, and the low may again approach or equal the low made at the last trend decline, but so long as this low holds, and is not broken, the major trend is, up. Although, this intervening minor trend is down. (See the period between Nov. 2-8, Nov. 9-21). A trader should use as his guide; the points, percentage move from last low, and the length of time the trend has been running, since the last important high or low—then be on the alert for the trend change signals.

When a major trend has been extended; with an active market, high prices, big price changes, with greatly increased volume; with a probable run of 1-2-3 days or more, with successive new highs; then those who sell at the sign of the "TR" rule will not get the top eighth, neither, will they have cause for regrets. (See Mar. 27-28-29, Dec. 4-5-6-7), The first heavy selling sinks the price; explained in latter pages. (A graphic or picture chart can be made from the trading-book and may help show this action better, however, the tabular font is more attention compelling for comparing volume, price changes, and the interpretation of the daily movement.)

When the zero or loss unit occurs, the result is a loss on the trade; to be consistent a trader is compelled to sell, in anticipation of an imminent decline from high of 2ⁿᵈ Selling Day, to low of Buying Day. (See Mar. 31 low to Apr. 2 high).

The Zero and "L" swings generally appear in downtrends; but when they occur in uptrends the loss is generally less than one-point. Out of each 100 successive (decline rally) 3 day swings examined; the loss swings occurred 12 times on an average. Of the total swing points, the loss points were about 3% of the gains.

This column will show the fluctuations in a stock, and whether the stock selected or trading the 3 day swings, has wide enough movement. Try other stocks.

THE (X) (√) ARE TREND INDICATORS

The "X" means the trading objective high or low was made FIRST.

The "√" means the trading objective high or low was made LAST.

These marks point the probable trend, prices, will take between the trading sessions—and are placed in the circles of a Buying Day and both Selling Days, at the close of the market.

The most important part of active trading; buying or selling, or buying stocks for trend trading (when buying you "fee;" your way into the market; at tops you sell in bulk—if you can) is to determine the trend of prices.

The Real Trend is the trend between the lows of buying days and the highs of selling days, and the trend to be determined, as distinguished from the many currents, smaller rallies and declines—for instance the low of day may be 50 and the established high 53, with the price trading between the two points as, 51 3/4. After these deviations the price will swing back to the real trend, through either 50 or 53, depending on the way the trend is headed. These fractional or point trends interfere and confuse a trader but do not change the ultimate direction of price toward the highs or lows the trading objectives.

(The uninformed trader buys into the market on a reaction or low point and by luck he hits the real trend just as the price starts to rally; then he sells with a few points profit, but on his next trade he buys or sells one of these cross-currents and the trade promptly shows a loss; not only, of the recently won gains, but it takes a "bite" out of his capital, and after a few trades of this kind he has a losing average.)

EXAMPLE OF OBJECTIVES MADE FIRST:

Suppose the price reacted from the high or 2nd Selling Day, then on the Buying Day made a low early in the session; then began to rally and traded the remainder of the session between the high and low, with the closing price nearer the high, than the low. The "X" would be placed in the Buying Day circle indicating the low was made FIRST. The trend at the close would be considered as, up. (See Oct. 30-31).

The opening of 1st Selling Day would generally be up and continue higher, with a probable penetration of the high or previous day. Then a decline, with a rally failing to reach the last high, with the close nearer the low. The selling objective would be made FIRST and an "X" placed in the 1st Selling Day circle. A trader would sell—at, and above the high of previous day—Buying Day—and would be out of the market, if he was using the 1st Selling Day as his objective. (See Nov. 1.).

EXAMPLE OF OBJECTIVES MADE LAST:

Suppose the price declined from high of 2nd Selling Day, made a low, then began to rally and closed up from this low, and at the opening, next day, was higher; making the high first on Buying Day; then declined during the remainder of the session with the close nearer the low of the day. The buying objective would be made LAST and a "√" placed in the Buying Day circle. The trend at the close would be considered as, down. (See April 2-3-4).

Suppose the low was made first on Buying Day, then rallied, with the close nearer the high of the day. The trend at the close would be considered as, up; at times the opening, next day, is down or opens at the previous closing price—this is due in part to a preponderance of "bunched" selling, over buying orders put in before the opening. After the opening the price holds or sells-off a little then rallies and makes the high of day. The "√" would be placed in the 1st Selling Day circle indicating that the high was made LAST. A trader would sell at this 'high on the penetration'—in this case—or failure to penetrate the high of previous day. (See Mar. 27-28)

When the buying and selling objectives are made FIRST, a trader is in-and-out without much delay, but when they are made LAST the move consumes more time and he must watch the entire trading session in order to complete the trade.

Trading would be easy if all FIRSTS and LASTS of the 3 day cycle were made, each in sequence, with penetrations. Unfortunately we get cycles of mixed symbols "X" and "√" with failures to penetrate at highs and lows of objective points, and these are caused by the cross-currents—detour trends—carrying over from one trading session into the next. Since a trader cannot make the market in a stock; (this is the job of the "Specialist" in a stock) he tries to follow it, and to anticipate the buying and selling—when and where—by the Specialist, on the trading floor of the Exchange.

BUYING DAY EXAMPLE:

At the opening of the market, notice whether the price was up and continued higher making the high FIRST, or whether it opened down and is declining further, making low FIRST. Making the high FIRST expect selling from this point and a reaction to follow on an up-opening, wait. Do not buy. Tape-traders don't buy on "bulges", they know a rally is limited and perhaps in the 3rd or 4th day up, from the last Buying Day low or under it. On a down-opening observe the spread from high of previous day, to low of present decline, and at this low, if the price is under the low of previous day. By checking back over the units in the "D" column a comparison can be made to determine the extent of this present decline, and gauged as a normal trading decline, or a severe reaction—perhaps following a change of trend.

The normal trading decline will generally stop; at, a little above or below the low of previous day—the low of 2nd Selling Day. The "buying spot" is around this low point when the activity quiets down and the trading becomes listless and dull. At times, the trading may be sort of "bouncy" above this low. Then again the decline may be precipitous, make a low, with a fast rally, then a slower decline falling short of the last low. From this low the rally often starts with each transaction decline failing to reach the last low, in other words, the price holds these small rally gains. From either of these kinds of lows, expect the rally to continue, which would show the real trend as, up.

The severe decline from high of previous day may continue throughout the Buying Day session, with little or no rally, with the closing price very near or on the low of day. This is a "flat" closing and the indications are for nearby further decline, in most cases, only occasionally is it profitable for the one day trader to buy a low made Last. Wait for the next Buying Day. Never start a trade in any case unless it favors your "play". (This is not so with the 3 day trader, who buys, then holds on through the intervening action, rallies and declines until his objective is reached—the high of 2nd Selling Day—where he sells with a profit, or loss.)

A SELLING DAY EXAMPLE:

When the low is made FIRST on a Buying Day, with the closing price nearer the high of the day; expect an up-opening, or higher prices, with a penetration of the high of previous day. Sell at-the-market—at, through and above this high. When using the 1st Selling Days the objective. (See Oct. 31 to Nov. 1).

(On either Selling Day, 1st or 2nd), should you sell too soon after a penetration you lose some of your probable profits. Expect not only slight but deeper penetrations of the highs, because the "tops" must be broken and be progressively higher in uptrend trading areas.

The activity of the market in the stock is a good sign to watch—whether increasing or decreasing on the rise, after penetration, also, after small "D" column decline units.)

From a high closing on Buying Day, when the opening next day is up, and with a wide gain; sell at-the-market, without waiting for the next transaction to appear on the tape, after the opening price. The price may go higher after you sell. So what? The opening price may be the high and is many times, and a decline may start from this high that could be the beginning of a down trend. (By so doing you get a profit and perhaps the major part of the rally.) (See Nov. 20 to 21).

From a high close of Buying Day; then should this gain at the close, be partly lost by a down-opening next day, or opens at the closing price of previous day; sell at-the-market without waiting for the next transactions on the tape. (See Dec. 5-6. Here 67 was made first; 70 1/2 LAST. Also March 27-28, here the low 88 7/8 was made first, at the opening, at the same price as previous close; 94 1/4 was made LAST). December 5 and March 27, were big intrasession rallies and experienced traders sell on an action of this kind, before the close; others put their orders in before the opening, next day, hoping to catch the top of the rally on a higher opening. Generally the price opens down or at the previous close, then rallies, when headed higher.

On wide up, or stalled openings, a trader acts immediately upon seeing the opening price. Should the following prices be up, his order is "in" and will be executed on the rising trend, and he gets a little more of the rally. Should the following prices be down he loses only part of his gain—his order is "in"—in time to "duck the real sell-off", and he will be out of the stock, and probably at the very inception of a declining trend. (Many traders at this point do nothing—if the price starts up after the opening, they wait to see what will happen; if it starts down they wait for a rally to "get-out—most likely the expected doesn't happen, either way, and the result is a greater loss.)

From the low of Buying Day there will be thousands of transactions on the tape between and before the price reaches the high of 2nd Selling Day—three sessions in the future—a trader using the 3 day swing, while interested in this action, will be more concerned with the action around the lows of Buying Days and the highs of 2nd Selling Days. (This is a more or less mechanical method of trading, but, the records show it to be profitable and a trader can win on balance, but the lot of the active trader is hard... the big money is in the big swings.) Northern Pacific Ry—(NP)—is used as an example, throughout, because it is representative of all the features required in a stock for active, intermediate, and primary trend trading—price appreciation. The illustrations show only the approach to highs and lows of the swings, that is, a few days prior to and after they have been made. The places of major and minor trend changes. Records can be obtained from back-number newspapers at any of the public libraries and a fill-in can be made of the entire movement in this stock.

The longer record will show the swings of a week or more, and where the pressure was applied, in a more or less degree, at tops, and support at bottoms, of these smaller movements. The trading characteristics remain the same, it's only a matter of extent of the movement—big or little.

The sole purpose is to point out a trading method—no "tip" is intended; a trader must make his own selections and he will find many stocks that are acceptable, if he will make-up a book on them and study it.

*From low 51¼ Oct. 27, to high 61¼ Nov. 21

From low 56¼ Nov. 26, to high 70½ Dec. 6

From high 70½ Dec. 6, to low 59 Feb. 5

From low 59 Feb. 5, to high 94⅜ Mar. 29

This drawing was started from Nov. 16, to concentrate the attention, to the action prior to and immediately after the high of an intermediary movement.

PLACE THIS SHEET ALONGSIDE PAGES FOR READY REFERENCE

TREND TRADERS

The Investor-Speculator, Intermediary and Primary trend traders have a means of buying or buying for accumulation; through the use of the Buying Day (observing the conditions around this point). In this way their buying is done around the low points of declines and not at tops of rallies, thus, saving many points—dollars. They would first determine the kind of market—bull or bear—and the price position of the stock in relation to the market as a whole.

It is not wise to try to buy a full line of stocks, all at once. Suppose the line was to be 100 or 500 shares or more—an order would be placed for part, say, 25 or 50 shares, at a time, in odd lots, to fill the former order and in round lots in proportion to the quantity wanted in the latter. After getting them he would wait until the next Buying Day; then place an order for another lot; continuing in this manner until completion of the full line.

This procedure would be a higher average cost, but each lot would be more apt to show a profit and he would have some assurance that he was following a rising trend.

Had he started his buying at a comparatively low range of prices and was in a rising market, it is not likely that he would be forced to carry a heavy load at a loss; in case of a sudden decline in the whole market.

At the determined time for selling he would be on the alert for the danger signals (explained next page), and in addition would have the use of the Selling Days (1st and 2nd).

Trading technique; is simply the ability through study, observation and experience, to detect the manipulation that takes place in the markets at all times, and to recognize the signals in each, of the several phases, of the market movement. The most important consideration for speculation, even ahead of earnings and dividends, is the technical position of the stock in relation to the market as a whole—leading or trailing—its position within its own group—leading or trailing—and the group attention in the news—

at this writing it is electronics.

Swing traders and semi-investors are more concerned with price appreciation, therefore, selection of a stock is of the utmost importance. Most of the stocks that make up the back-bone of the market are in the conservative class and trading profits should be figured on a percentage basis and not on points. The trader who will do a little retrospective research will find that many stocks he may have in mind are not suitable for his style of trading. Get the highs and lows of the one or more sustained swings that a stock makes each year and then figure the percentage gains and losses of the rally and decline swings, from lows to highs and highs to lows. The Market Averages may show great gains and losses up and down, in points, with a percentage gain or loss of an individual stock disappointingly small.

A trader buying stocks around any low point, Bear Bottoms or Secondary Reactions in a Bull Market (here he should use the 3 day rule for accumulation) should carefully check the percentage rise of his stock as the price moves up from the low point but most important: a stock that is going up will do so with but small and normal set-backs until it reaches the high of the move, regardless of percentages, so the trader must be constantly on the alert for the day when his stock will make top—in many cases this top will be made quite unexpectedly but not without warning. Watch the build-up of the volume for a few days prior to the top and the greatly reduced volume the next and for a few days after or the volume might remain large for a few days before and after the high is made. The decrease in volume is caused by a let-up in the selling pressure for technically the stock may not be able to withstand further heavy selling without breaking the prices, too much. Many times a trading range is formed between the high and the low of the break-back and the stock will trade in this range indefinitely, weeks and months, depending on the strength or weakness of the general market—further distribution takes place in this range and on the way down, if, the general market is headed that way. This phenomenon of the action of individual stocks is a feature of the market prior to bull market endings—with one stock after another refusing to participate in any further rise in the market, while the general market continues to advance—this same action takes place in a lesser degree before severe intermediate declines. This may not be the action of low priced late movers, that move up fast, make a top and start to decline, seldom going back to their highs a second time. Being behind, they must hustle to catch up with the general market which is plainly showing a declining tendency.

This sudden reaching of the top on greatly increased volume compared with the previous daily totals, then, a slight break of several percent of price from the high while the volume continues large, is the results of heavy selling, mixed with public buying and inside short selling, caused perhaps by advance in information adversely affecting the stock;—sufficient to cause large profit taking or the price is deemed high enough to begin distribution or the stock. Regardless of the reason, this action definitely warns the trader that the intent is not to put the price higher, at least not for the present—and is his signal to—the market is broad enough at these, times to take the selling and is the opportune time to turn paper profits into cash.

The lows points of Bull Market Secondary Reactions are just the reverse of the top action; the low many times is made on relatively heavy volume, then a rally for a day or two, and a further decline on very tight volume with the price holding above the last low point, with trading dull, (established points at either highs or lows may be penetrated slightly by the trading that takes place but are not sufficient reason to withhold selling or buying at these points.) The short seller on this trend must be on the alert or this same big day, only on the downside; for then the stock is in supply or covering short sales, and is the long stock bought at higher prices, now, being sold at the bottom.

The market action for swing trading is identically the same as that used for the 3 day method, only on an enlarged scale. The minor movement receives the same support on the declines and is subjected to the same pressure on the rallies.

With the selection of the stock, it is only good judgment to get a report on the company, its past and future probabilities—but, unless the market action of the stock confirms the report a trader should let it alone—watch but don't buy. The time for buying should be based solely on the technical indications and the present market position, in relation to the low and high for the year. It could be selling so near to a top (temporarily, perhaps), that by waiting a short time it can be bought at a wide concession. Most all Bull markets show at least one or more important declines during the year that buying opportunities, but the most important part is; starting at exactly the right time. A decline in a stock, due to a general decline in the market as a whole, is not of great concern but the way it acts on the rally, and the preparations for a new move is important. A trader should look for buying in a stock around the lows of important declines—after the market stabilizes. It takes considerable buying to start a stock up and continuous buying to keep it going up. Many good stocks lack trading appeal, sponsorship, or due to other conditions, move with such sluggish action that they are unattractive to the more active traders.

Stocks with a good future potential should be watched but a trader should not wait until "they make the news" before buying—at this time they might be a better sale. Buying in a stock shows, in the way the stock acts. He should follow the progress of a stock; at bottoms or where it begins to form a well defined horizontal trend—confined to a narrow trading range—and trades on a fair amount of volume and activity, with some fair size lots or stock. He then waits for a day of unusual activity and volume and gets ready to buy at the very inception of the "break out" of this range, top side. He will buy part of his stock at this point—then wait for a reaction to see how it acts on this decline and to confirm his judgment, whether, he was right in buying the first lot. He then buys more after the stock rallies and just as it makes a new high. His buying is done in this manner, because, at times, the stock may turn and go in the opposite direction, and may "dip" low enough to break the line of lows at the bottom of this range. (An action of this kind "cleans up all the stops" below the line of bottom prices and "shakes off" a following before the real move gets under way.) Having acquired his stock he holds on for the move; an indefinite period perhaps three to six months or longer, or until he recognizes the described action around tops.

In some years there are no well defined lines at bottoms. Stocks begin their advance from other trading ranges. Bottoms of long declines may be reached by a particular violent downward thrust—establish a low—generally followed by an immediate sharp rally and a subsequent slower decline on a greatly reduced volume and activity—stopping short of the last low. A trader does not try to buy long stock on this fast decline—he waits for the "quiet-spot" on the reaction after the rally—and when the market becomes "dull". He will buy part of his line at this point (with the intent to sell-out should the stock make a new low); then add to it where the stock begins to make new highs, in series. In case he is forced to sell, he starts over again from a new low—using this same action. (The manner of buying at bottoms—shows why—he should not expect to get less than a 10% average above extreme lows.)

A stock that trades in listless manner on a very small volume; with intermittent small transactions, with absent days of trading, shows neglect; and no immediate interest, and should not be bought until it shows a more active participation in the market. A trader recognizing this action in a stock should look to the company report for the reason. A stock must be traded in fair size lots and volume in order to accumulate it.

Experienced traders and tape readers, can generally distinguish a rally from a change in trend by figuring how far a stock should come back, allowing that a normal rally is from one-half to two-thirds of the decline. In the case the decline is not over, the rally will fall short. The large transactions will be on the downside and the smaller lots on the upside. The volume is light and the activity "fades-away" with the rally "dying out" at the top. Where the trend is

to continue the trading shows a steady rise on increasing volume and demand for the stock, and where there is an urgent demand for stock for 'short covering" the pace will be accelerated. The large transactions are on the upside and are taken at the higher prices, with the smaller transactions on the downside. (This same action can be seen in the smallest daily—in the broader and longer movements—and in the Market Averages.)

Many stocks make two tops—the Real and Actual—the Real Top is where the first heavy liquidation takes place after long advances; then, after a decline of a week or more, a rally or continuation of the advance, many times, will exceed the first high making the Actual Top on a volume as large—more or less. A trader should be on the alert to begin his selling the instant he detects this inside selling. (The point here is; he must sell when he has a market, if his holdings are large). Experienced traders take their profits at this point and do not try to anticipate an Actual Top (which may or may not happen). The high made on this kind of action may be one and the same—the Real and Actual. When this does happen the stock makes a new high and has a tendency to make the ordinary traders intensely bullish—they continue to "hold on" or 'come in" as new buyers—to take the stock at, perhaps, top prices. (And this is just what is expected of them.)

The Real Top, is generally one or several days of advancing prices after a long move up, culminating (Or with a quick, sharp, upward thrust on abnormally large volume and activity, compared to previous trading). The stock; makes a high then resists all further buying—the supply and demand comes into balance—with the trading very active [or] sustained—but the stock makes little or no progress either way. The heavy selling at this point is, temporarily discontinued, but the "selling sources" continue to force a little more stock on the market than can be absorbed, causing this sagging decline, on greatly reduced daily volume. Near or at the low of this decline there is a noticeable increase in the volume for a day or more—the stock must be bought in large enough quantities to absorb all selling and turn the stock up. The day of heaviest support is the Real Bottom, then, many times after a short sub-normal rally or series of rallies, the stock may sell just a little lower on a negligible amount of volume—making the Actual Bottom—before the rally or uptrend is resumed. (A new high has a bullish effect and causes buying. A new low has a bearish effect and causes traders to sell out at bottoms, or at least, refrain from buying.)

A trader will repurchase a small part of his stock "as a trading lot" near this first decline low in anticipation of a rally or on the assumption that an uptrend will extend far enough to make a new and Actual Top. (But, with the firm resolve to re-sell at, through, and above this new high—or to "get-out-quick"—if after a rally, the reaction breaks the last or support low).

There are other stocks that make one top— the Real and actual—and on comparatively light volume, with no signs indicating that a top has been reached. The long decline starts with a series of small reactions and rallies but with a definite downward tendency. These tops are difficult to recognize. (If, in fact, they can be.) A trader should understand the characteristics of these stocks or at least have some idea of the percentage appreciation or number of points in the swings of the past years, as a guide to the future—and he should be satisfied to sell, if and when, past results as good or better can be attained. In this case a stock that fails to make a new high in a reasonable period of time should be sold, particularly so, if other stocks in the market are showing the heavy top action. (The trader who can recognize these diverse movements in the market can use them as confirmation of this weakened technical condition of the market as a whole.)

A trader who will start right—buy and sell accordingly to these "age old" tenets—will find little need for many of these "new discoveries" and other "wearisome" statistical market indices.

SUPPLEMENTARY ARTICLES

LINDA BRADFORD RASCHKE'S
TAYLOR'S SWING TRADING METHOD

REPRINTED WITH PERMISSION FROM CLUB 3000 NEWS, A PUBLICATION OF CLUB 3000 (FROM ISSUE #93.19, DECEMBER 30, 1993)

We heartily recommend Club 3000 to any readers who are interested in joining a "Futures Traders Network," whose members share information with each other on such topics as books, software, system design, testing, development and implementation, and many other areas of interest through a periodic newsletter:

B.A. "BO" THUNMAN
CLUB 3000
4550 N 38TH ST.
AUGUSTA, MI 49012
PHONE AND FAX (616) 713-5600

I have organized much of my trading methodology and philosophy around short-term techniques, as defined by George Douglass Taylor and thus have recommended his book *The Taylor Trading Technique*, as one well worth studying. However, Taylor was definitely a better trader than author! Here are some pointers from which to approach the book:

First, read the chapter Pertinent Points two or three times; this makes a much better introduction to the subject matter. Skip chapters 2,3, and 4 completely. I do not make up a "book' as Taylor does, nor do I recommend doing so. I do write down the open, high, low and close and underline the 3 to 4 day swing lows and swing highs. It helps to keep some type of log by hand, it keeps trading "systematic".

Where Taylor discusses various *Buy Day or Sell Day concepts*, I find it useful to diagram examples in the margin, using candlesticks. I also find it helpful to read his book with a yellow highlighter handy. In fact, I have gone through several copies because they keep getting so marked up.

Think in terms of concepts instead of specifics. These concepts, include: Trading within a 2 to 3 day time frame; price action around the previous day's high/low; the length of the upswing relative to the downswing; ignoring all news and fundamentals—concentrating strictly on what tape or price action is telling you. That is the only "truth" in short-term trading.

Keep in mind that Taylor's particular labels for each day were just his way of staying systematic, simple and consistent. If you read between the lines, you'll see his specific rules for shorting on "buy" days and buying on "sell short" days—it really has to do with how many days up/down the market is from the previous swing low/high.

Though trading on a 1- to 2-day basis, *be conscious of the bigger picture*—even Taylor said to skip the first "buy" trade when breaking down out of a congestion area. In other words, wait five to six days before looking to buy, instead of two or three. He also emphasized the importance of overall long-term and seasonal trends. Understanding markets includes recognizing when price is discounted and when marked up and watching for signs of support by interests larger than ourselves.

I have found that some of the most successful mechanical systems/price patterns/ methodologies work because they use the concept of "in one day, out the next". Examples include Larry Williams' patterns, Bob Buran's methodology and Toby Crabel's studies. *Enter on a trigger or pivot, exit on the next day's opening or close.*

I test patterns on a close-to-close basis—enter on a close, exit on a close one or two days later. My systems have no more than two parameters. They are crude models that highlight a market's tendency. For instance, "selling a higher opening after two higher closes" illustrates a market's tendency to pull back at that point,

My market models indicate whether the odds favor being a buyer or a seller for the day. I then use Taylors "rules" to trade as if it is a "buy day" or a "sell short" day. I hold the trade overnight and exit according to his guidelines. Don't carry losing positions overnight, it is better to exit with the intention of re-entering at a better trade location the next trading day.

I first came across Taylor's name In George Angell's book, *Winning in the Futures Market*, specifically the chapter referring to the "LSS Method".

After studying Taylor's book for a more comprehensive understanding of his guidelines, I first adapted his techniques for S&P trading. Taylor emphatically teaches students of his techniques that they must never average down. I have yet to come across a consistent, winning trader who practices this most destructive of habits. One may get away with averaging a loser, but doing so will add much more volatility to your bottom line and, sooner or later, be your undoing. It is very difficult to be in the proper frame of mind for trading when carrying losing positions on a daily statement. Many of Taylor's rules are, in fact, defensive in nature—for example, exiting on the first reaction when a market does not act "correctly".

Following Taylor's guidelines diligently should develop within you the best possible trading "habits". Ultimately, it is one's trading habits which govern one's success.

George Angell's
Winning in the Futures Market: A Money Making Guide to Trading, Hedging, and Speculating
(*Revised Edition*)

Chapter 13 "The LSS 3-day Cycle Method: A Day-Trading Approach to the Markets" Reprinted with permission.

This book is published by:

Probus Publishing Company

1925 N. Clybourne Avenue

Chicago, IL 60614

Given the volatility, pace, and high leverage of today's futures markets, it is surprising that more traders don't take this approach. Day trading, as the name suggests, is simply the completion of the round-turn, in-and-out buy and sell cycle within a single trading session.

The method is popular among traders for several reasons. First and foremost is the issue of safety. If you are not in the market overnight, nothing troublesome is going to happen to you on tomorrow's open. You'd be surprised how suddenly a seemingly profitable trade at yesterday's close can go sour on today's open. All you need is a little news overnight or an unexpected money-supply report. The damage to the unwary can be awesome. Second, day trading has reduced margin requirements. If you aren't holding a position overnight, chances are excellent you won't have a margin call. That is not to say, of course, that you can totally avoid losing trades. You can't. But the combination of no overnight jitters, no margin calls, and an overall relaxed method of rapid in-and-out trading can do wonders for the spirit.

In recent years, there has been a trend toward day trading among public speculators. To see how popular this form of trading has become, you only have to look at the volume and open interest statistics for the popular S&P 500 contract. On an average day, the volume will be twice the open interest—about sixty thousand contracts traded against about half that number held in open positions overnight. This represents a significant amount of in-and-out trading.

For years, professional floor traders relied on day trading—often, a specialized form of day trading known as scalping, in which small profits are taken over and over again throughout the day—for a very understandable reason: the professionals know the risks of holding onto a futures too long. Unlike the public trader, the floor trader, who is a member of an exchange, doesn't pay commissions. As a result, the floor traders do not have to worry about commission costs. Nevertheless, the real reason that the professionals concentrate on small, yet profitable, moves is due to the risk involved. For the trader who holds a position for a week or more, one mistake and he's finished. In contrast, the day trader can be wrong five or six times during the day and still emerge a winner.

Since today's discounted commissions are lower than ever before, the public speculator can now join in the fray with those specialized in-and-out traders down on the floor. It is still almost impossible to truly scalp from the outside, but day trading, in which you might take two or three trades during the day, is something else again. Down on the floor, a trader who just does two or three trades is considered a position trader—like someone who holds a position for three months on the outside. So it is truly a matter of perspective.

THE POTENTIAL FOR PROFITS

Another reason why day trading has become popular is the genuine potential for profits. In today's volatile markets, where the value of a single contract may move up or down by a couple of thousand dollars during a single trading session, the potential for profits is considerable. When viewed in this fashion, the cost of a $20 commission suddenly becomes negligible. Large, aggressive floor traders in the volatile S&P pit can occasionally make six figures in a single trading session. So don't be put off when someone says "What do you want to take 'small' profits for?" The answer is very simple. Because you want to be around to trade tomorrow. And, what's more, because you would like to grow rich in the process!

You hear so often that the serious money in futures is made on the so-called "big moves." What you don't hear about is the road to the big move—the days and even weeks in adversity when the really big traders have to finance their losing positions to the tune of millions of dollars. Clearly, the answer for the novice or small trader is to try day trading.

One rule if you are going to be successful at day trading is to select the right market. On this score, you want a market that both enjoys a wide participation and has sufficient volatility, to enable you to extract profits. A few years ago, you might have selected the gold market, which was second only to Treasury bonds in both participation and volatility. In those days, $15 and even $20 moves were common in the gold market. No more. Today, the gold market struggles to move $3.00 or $4.00 a day.

The selection of the market will be determined by economic conditions at the time you decide to trade. During inflationary periods and a weak dollar, expect gold and silver to prove volatile. But, at other times, you will have to look elsewhere. A glance at a recent newspaper shows that nearby Standard & Poor's 500 futures had a daily range of 1.70 points ($850 per contract) and nearby U.S. Treasury bonds had a daily range of 26/32 ($812 per contract). In contrast, during the same trading session, corn moved two and a quarter cents ($112 per contract) and oats even less, just a penny and a quarter ($62 per contract). Obviously, the S&P and bonds are better day-trading vehicles.

To find a good day-trading candidate, select only markets that have depth (liquidity) and volatility. Otherwise, you are going to be disappointed in your trading results. Recently, the stock index, interest rate, and currency futures have all offered worthwhile day-trading opportunities. One other word of advice: Try to stay with the leading futures of each group. That would mean the S&P, Treasury bond, and Deutschemark in the three respective groups listed above.

In recent years, the focus has shifted away from the agricultural commodities toward the newer financial futures. Given a resurgence in the agricultural sector, day traders may again find soybeans, among the grains, and pork bellies, among the meats, worthwhile day-trading vehicles.

TAYLOR'S BOOK METHOD—THE GENESIS OF A TRADING SYSTEM

During the nineteen fifties, a little-known grain trader at the Chicago Board of Trade published a manual known as the Book Method. The trader, George Douglas Taylor, maintained that the grain markets moved in a three-day cycle that could be tracked by measuring the rallies and declines. Taylor kept a record of grain prices and their respective rallies and declines in a notebook he carried with him—hence the title Book Method. What is remarkable today is how accurate this simple bookkeeping entry can be when applied to the markets of the eighties.

Although the grain markets of the fifties were far from turbulent, Taylor observed what he came to call "market engineering." He found a pattern in the market. By painstakingly recording the magnitude of market rallies and declines, which he kept in his notebook, Taylor found a three-day cycle that, despite occasional aberrations, repeated itself over and over again.

What's more, Taylor maintained that the natural rhythm of the market created a false move that served to fool traders into buying when they should be selling, and vice versa. The powers in the grain markets, Taylor maintained, frequently caused prices to decline in order to create a buying opportunity for themselves; within three days, after the market had rallied sufficiently to provide them with handsome profits, a short-term top was created in order to provide a selling opportunity. This was the market "engineering" at work. Although the pattern had remained hidden, with sufficient research and careful examination of prices, one could uncover these precise buying and selling opportunities. For anyone who has ever sought to utilize a trading system, this was powerful information.

Ironically, Taylor's method wasn't a day-trading technique at all—undoubtedly, given the ranges of those days, one would be hard put to pull day-trading profits out of the market—but a short-term trading system in which positions were held overnight. He gave a name to each trading day: the Buy Day, the Sell Day, and the Short Sale Day. Each day had its particular trading characteristic. For instance, the Buy Day was identified as the day in which prices either open at or retreat to a low prior to rising. The Sell Day, in turn, was characterized by prices trading at, below, or slightly above the previous day's high. And on the Short Sale Day the market took a final lunge upward, which was met by selling resistance, and prices broke. Then the cycle began all over again.

Although the notion of a three-day cycle, with the precise pattern described above, is highly simplistic, it has the elements of an idea that deserved attention. It meant that if indeed such a cycle did exist, and if one could successfully "read" the hidden intentions of the market at specific stages, then perhaps one could successfully trade from the winning side. Moreover, it posed several important questions. When is a rally not a rally, but, rather, a skillful attempt to lure buyers into a trap? Conversely, when is a price break simply a ruse to create selling to provide the powerful interests an opportunity to buy at low prices? Obviously, if one could indeed learn the hidden signals of the market, one's opportunity to profit would surely increase.

THE BOOK METHOD
THIRTY YEARS LATER

Over the years, the Book Method, which was self-published in notebook form, has become an underground classic of sorts among futures traders. Few copies are available, and those that can be found in trading libraries are dog-eared and well worn.

Unfortunately, Taylor's advice was exceedingly general. You should sell on the third day's rally at, through, or slightly below the previous day's high. You should buy on the following day, following a break in prices at, through, or slightly above the previous day's low. These, essentially, were his rules. Often, they were vague and hard to identify. Where do you buy? At a higher bottom (a very bullish sign, according to Taylor) or somewhere under the previous day's low? Do you always sell on the third day's rally?

Determining the cycle itself becomes problematic. While the three-day cycle is at the heart of the system, Taylor hedged and said that occasionally you will find a four- or five-day cycle. Well, how do you know when the longer cycle is occurring? And if you are selling on the third day's rally, what should you do with your short position while prices are rising? The answers to these and other questions remain inconclusive. At times, the cycle will change. And when the market breaks, you will have a sense of so-called Buy Days in which lower lows are made daily. Which is the correct low to establish the Buy Day?

Despite these and other persistent questions about the Book Method, the basic pattern can be observed in a number of futures contracts—among them the metals, interest rates, and stock index futures, as well as the grains. What's more, the pattern seems even more identifiable among these newer financial futures than among the more traditional grain contracts. What's the pattern? How do you identify it? And, most important, how can you make money trading the three-day cycle as a day trader?

THE IDEAL THREE-DAY PATTERN

The ideal three-day pattern, which Taylor first identified, consists of the Buy Day, in which the low is established first and the market trades higher; the Sell Day, in which the Buy Day high is considered as a resistance point; and a third day, the Short Sale Day, in which the high of the Sell Day is challenged or taken out prior to a retreat in prices—at which point the cycle begins over again. The three-day pattern is illustrated in Figure 49 in which the horizontal ticks to the left and right respectively indicate the open and close. Note that the second day, or Sell Day, is an immediate day during which the market gains strength to challenge the high on the following day, the Short Sale Day—which, according to Taylor, is the day on which the market "engineering" works to fool the unwary that the market is indeed headed higher and create the ideal selling opportunity.

There is a paradox at work here that thoughtful traders should be mindful of when they place their orders:

1. The market is often taken down, in order to create selling, to provide a safe buying opportunity for the powerful market forces (see Figure 50).

2. The market is often taken up, in order to create buying, to provide a safe selling opportunity for the powerful market forces (see Figure 51).

THE ORDER IN WHICH THE HIGH AND LOW OCCUR

When identifying the three-day pattern, Taylor was careful to make a note on whether the high or the low occurred first during the trading day. He marked the low on Buy Days and the highs on Sell Days and Short Sale Days. If the low occurred first on the Buy Day, he would indicate this with an X (we've used an asterisk on our examples); if the low occurred last, he would place a check (we've used a double asterisk). On the Sell Days or Short Sale Days, he would place an X if the high occurred first and place a check if the high occurred last.

The order in which each occurred was vital to the smooth functioning of his system, because when the high or low occurred out of sequence—that is, when the reverse was expected—he would often find that he could push the cycle ahead a day and the three-day pattern would again become evident.

In the table below, you will find price data on a recent contract of Standard & Poor's 500 futures. You should note which numbers are underlined and whether an asterisk or a double asterisk is indicated.

Note that there are three Buy Days over this ten-day period. They are as follows: Wednesday, August 21; Monday, August 26; and Thursday, August 29. On each Buy Day, the low is underlined; on each Sell Day and Short Sale Day, the high is underlined. The asterisks in the Buy Days mean the low was made first during the trading session; the asterisks in the Sell Days and Short Sale Days mean the high was made first during the trading session. The double asterisk signifies that the underlined number was achieved last during the trading session.

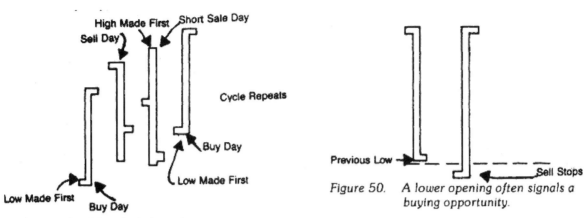

Figure 49.   The ideal three-day pattern.

Figure 50.   A lower opening often signals a buying opportunity.

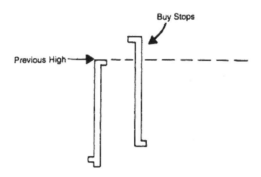

Figure 51. A high opening often signals a selling opportunity.

Standard & Poor's 500

September 1985

Date	Open	High	Low	Close
Aug 19 - Mon.	186.80	**187.80	186.70	187.40
Aug 20 - Tues.	188.00	**189.50	187.80	189.35
Aug 21 - Wed.	189.50	190.30	*189.00	189.75
Aug 22 - Thurs.	190.00	**190.10	187.55	187.90
Aug 23 - Fri.	187.80	*187.90	186.85	187.40
Aug 26 - Mon.	186.80	188.15	*186.30	188.05
Aug 27 - Tues.	188.30	*188.65	187.80	188.35
Aug 28 - Wed.	188.25	**188.70	187.85	188.45
Aug 29 - Thurs.	188.45	188.80	*188.15	188.75
Aug 30 - Fri.	188.55	*188.90	187.55	187.90

HOW TO IDENTIFY THE THREE-DAY CYCLE

The rule for identifying the three-day pattern is as follows: Take ten days of data and circle the lowest low of the ten days. This is the Buy Day. Then count forward and back, circling the two highs in both directions. Every third day becomes the Buy Day.

As you can see in the table above, the lowest low occurred on Monday, August 26. This is the Buy Day. Would the next day in the sequence be a Buy, Sell, or Short Sale Day? The next day would be the Sell Day, or the second day in the three-day cycle. The one-two-three-day cycle pattern then repeats as it has in the table.

You will note that on all three Buy Days, the low was made first during the trading session. You can see that Wednesday, August 21, was the day to buy at the low made first. The third day, Friday, August 23, was the Short Sale Day with the high made first—the ideal three-day cycle. Although Friday's price was indeed lower then Wednesday's, the pattern persisted nevertheless. That is, you could have sold soon after the open on Friday, August 23, and made money, because the open was very close to the high of the day.

There are many more inferences to be drawn from the table of prices. For instance, while you could have purchased the low made first on Monday, August 26, three days later the reverse proved true. The high was made after the low, or last during the trading session. As a result, a short sale near the open on Wednesday, August 28, would not have been a good point to sell.

Before moving on to a more advanced concept, you should practice identifying the three-day pattern. First, you circle the lowest low of the past ten days and then count forward and back. Which is the Buy Day? The Sell Day? The Short Sale Day? Tomorrow's day is always identified by the previous day. Thus, if today is the Buy Day, expect the Sell Day to occur tomorrow. And so on.

KEEPING THE BOOK

Once you can identify the pattern, you can begin keeping the book. The book is at the heart of Taylor's system—and, as we shall see in the section on the worksheet, at the heart of the LSS 3-day Cycle Method as well. But before we can get to the LSS system, we should concentrate on what Taylor said.

Essentially, Taylor was a believer in measuring the rallies and declines. His was a percentage method in which he attempted to see how far a rally or decline tended to carry. Once it was measured, he could pinpoint changes in the market—and, more important, he could estimate how far a rally or decline was likely to carry.

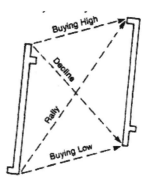

Figure 52. *Taylor measured four key rally and decline figures as shown above.*

Taylor made four key measurements—all of which have been incorporated into the LSS system as well. Illustrated in Figure 52, the measurements quantify the following:

1. The Decline column (D)—Difference between previous day's high and today's low
2. The Rally column (R)—Difference between previous day's low and today's high
3. The Buying High column (BH)—Difference between today's high and previous day's high
4. The Buying Under column (BU)—Difference between today's low and previous day's low

Standard & Poor's 500

September 1985

Date	Open	High	Low	Close	D	R	BH	BU
July 22—Mon.	196.20	196.35	**194.25	195.45				
July 23—Tues.	195.75	*196.50	193.25	193.55	3.10	2.25	.15	1.00
July 24—Wed.	193.55	*193.75	191.60	191.90	4.90	.50	− 2.75	1.70
July 25—Thurs.	192.30	193.00	*191.95	192.90	1.80	1.40	− .75	− .35
July 26—Fri.	192.80	*193.45	192.30	192.85	.70	1.50	.45	− .35
July 29—Mon.	192.50	*192.55	189.70	189.75	3.75	.25	− .90	2.60
July 30—Tues.	189.95	191.05	*189.60	190.50	2.95	1.35	− 1.50	.10

Note: *means that the highs and lows were made first during the trading session

**signifies a high or low being achieved last during the trading session

Actually, Taylor included a fifth measurement which was identical to the Buying High column. He gave it a different name because he used it on only one day during the cycle and not on the other two. In the interest of simplicity, this fifth column has been dropped. Moreover, since every measurement is taken every day, it would be redundant as well.

The best way to learn to keep the book is by example. In the following table we have listed the open, high, low, and close of seven trading days in the September 1985 S&P futures contract. From these prices, we have calculated the respective Decline, Rally, Buying High, and Buying Under column numbers. Make sure you understand how each number is calculated before moving on.

Consider the entries for Wednesday, July 24. On that day, the Short Sale Day, the market opened near its high and promptly sold off, completing the ideal three-day pattern and setting up an opportunity to go long on the following day at the low made first. Looking to the right, you'll see that the entry in the Decline column was 4.90. This is the total range between the previous day's high and the just completed day's low. The rally entry on that day was just .50 points, the difference between the previous day's low and the next day's high. Looking at the Buying High entry, you'll see that a negative number appears. When this occurs, you know the day's high is below the previous day's high, since the formula is today's high minus yesterday's high equals the RH column entry. Lastly, the Buying Under column shows a positive number, because today's low was lower than the previous day's low. This column measures how far under the previous day's low the market traded. In this instance, the market traded precisely 1.70 points under the previous low.

Incidentally, on the day shown, you have the makings of an excellent buying opportunity on the following day. First, you'll notice you have the classic Short Sale Day pattern: high made first and then a break in the market with the close near the low. Second, you have the Buy Day occurring on the following day. The anticipated pattern, therefore, is for the market to rally—low made first and then up. Moreover, Taylor mentioned that the very strongest buying opportunity presented itself when you had the opportunity to buy a higher low. This means the low on the previous Short Sale Day holds and is never penetrated. Indeed, this is precisely what occurred. The low at 191.60 holds and the market rallies off the 191.95 point the following day and closes near the top end of the range. Over the next three days, the entire cycle repeats itself.

Before we move on, let's look at some more entries. Look at the entry in the BU column on Tuesday, July 30. The .10 entry means the market traded just .10 points under the previous day's low. Had it held a higher bottom, the number would have been negative, since you are taking today's low and subtracting yesterday's low.

How about the Buying High entry on Monday, July 29? Negative .90 points. This is the amount under the previous day's high where today's high occurred. A negative Buying High number means today's high is under yesterday's.

THE LSS 3-DAY CYCLE METHOD

So far, we've looked at the basics of Taylor's Book Method: finding the cycle, keeping the book, and so on. But, at this point, Taylor becomes somewhat vague. Where do you buy and sell? Taylor says, at the Buy Day low made first. This position is then liquidated on the following day, the Sell Day. Where? At, through, or slightly below the previous day's high. On the third day, the Short Sale Day, the Book Method calls for taking short sales on the high made first. Ideally, this will occur at, through, or slightly below the Sell Day high.

There are several problems with Taylor's instructions. First, how do you quantify the buying and selling points? Do you, for instance, take the entry in the previous day's Rally column and use that number to extrapolate a price at which to sell? Perhaps. Second, what exactly does at, through, or slightly below the previous day's high mean? Fifty points, a hundred points? Again, it is hard to say. While Taylor's theory appears sound, a more quantifiable approach is required. Lastly, the market doesn't announce whether a price is the high or low made first. During the trading day, when you are faced with a decision, you cannot tell whether what appears, say, as a low made first might not be, indeed, a high made first. So, there are clearly problems

with Taylor's method.

In order to develop a system that would stand up to extensive computer analysis, it was necessary to develop rules that could be tested against the past. The rules couldn't be vague. They had to be specific. This has given rise to the LSS 3-day Cycle Method in its present form.

While the three-day cycle notion appears sound, the LSS system has refined the idea and incorporated a number of computer-proven ideas that Taylor never used.

For one, the LSS system is strictly a day-trading method. During Taylor's day, the grain markets rarely moved sufficiently to have a day-trading method that would work. Today, all that is changed. Soybeans can move 30 cents within a given trading session, and the stock index futures have no limits at all. Profits of three or four thousand dollars in a day's time are not uncommon on even a modest position for today's trader.

For another, the LSS system relies on a tier approach to putting on positions. Whereas Taylor tried to quantify trading days as better than others, the LSS system relies on letting the market decide the number of positions to take. There are three levels of trading. On any given day, you may take none or all three levels. The number of contracts taken at each level is the same. Although margin considerations and one's bankroll should determine the size of one's commitment in the market, the system was tested on a 3-3-3 contract basis. That is, during the day, you might have a maximum of three, six, or nine contracts. At day's end, of course, you will liquidate your entire position, win or lose. In this fashion, you will either profit or lose during the day. No positions are ever held over-night.

DEVELOPING A CONSENSUS

Taylor had the right idea. There is a three-day cycle. It occurs on a regular basis. And it is identifiable. But the secret of market success isn't as easy as buying every third day—far from it. In reality, the market often gets out of "phase" and the cycle often becomes lost to the would-be three-day cycle trader. As a result, the low often doesn't hold on the Buy Day. Instead, the market breaks. And the buyer often has losses.

To cope with the unpredictability of the market, an element of flexibility had to be built into the system. To avoid confusion, the notion of Buy, Sell, and Short Sale days had to be dispensed with—at least, the names had to be changed, because one often gets confused when selling, for example, on the so-called Buy Day. This is where the LSS designation becomes important. The LSS really should read: L-S-SS, the letters standing for "long," "sell," "short sale." But the point is simple: You can either buy or sell on any given day. Don't let the name or letters confuse you.

The LSS system, which is based on computer-proven probabilities and percentages, is designed to react to market conditions as they unfold during the day. For instance, if computer studies indicate that the probabilities of a buying position on any given day are 75 percent in favor of its working as opposed to just 25 percent of its losing, you are better off buying. To establish the probabilities, the system relies on calculating averages, and averages of averages, and mixing them all together to come up with a trading recommendation—again, in response to actual market conditions. The market decides whether and when you buy and sell. As a result, the system is much more reliable than any forecasting method.

Computer studies have shown that 70 percent of all LSS winners are made by short selling. That's better than two to one in favor of a short-selling position working over a buying position. Actually, to an experienced futures trader, this shouldn't come as a surprise. As a rule, most public speculators are buyers—not sellers. Moreover, the vast majority of all futures traders end up with losses. This suggests that although there is indeed a buyer for every seller, there are many, many more buyers, in number, than sellers. That is, a relatively small pool of sellers routinely fades the buying public.

If you monitor price action over a period of time, you'll notice that price breaks tend to be considerably faster than price rallies. Again, this phenomenon suggests that the "herd" of buyers all panic and stampede for the exits at once. This is precisely what happens when the stops are run. First, the very thinly bankrolled traders run (and the knowledgeable few who are simply on the wrong side), then the stops are hit and, as the market breaks, larger and larger long-term traders begin to bail out of their positions. By the time the public funds are selling, you know the bottom has been reached. This familiar price action has been likened to rolling a large boulder up a mountain. It goes up very slowly. But once you push it off the cliff it breaks fast! The same thing is true in the market. And it explains why the short side of the market is so profitable.

THE TREND REACTION NUMBERS

As part of the consensus, the system relies on the trend-reaction buy number and the trend-reaction sell number. These numbers are but one of four numbers that will be used to calculate the buy and sell envelopes that are so important to the LSS system. While the trend-reaction buy and sell numbers are often surprisingly close to the bottom and top of the day's range, respectively, they are not to be used as buying and selling points.

The formula for calculating the buy and sell numbers is as follows:

$$\frac{\text{High} + \text{Low} + \text{Close}}{3} = x$$

2x - high = trend-reaction buy number

2x - low = trend-reaction sell number

Assume the following:

S&P futures high = 189.55

" " low = 187.75

" " close = 188.25

Using the numbers listed above, the trend-reaction buy and sell would be calculated as follows:

$$\frac{189.55 + 187.75 + 188.25}{3} = 188.50$$

2(188.50) - 189.55 = 187.45 = trend-reaction buy number

2(188.50) - 187.75 = 189.25 = trend-reaction sell number

REPHASING THE CYCLE

Taylor's rule for generating the cycle days is to take ten days of price data, take the lowest low, and call it the Buy Day, and then count forward and backward, circling the third low and the two intermediate highs. In this manner, the three-day cycle is determined. Unfortunately, this approach is too inflexible to take into account the many crosscurrents in the market. Even Taylor maintained that the three-day cycle was occasionally interrupted by a four- or five-day cycle. Moreover, where one begins the cycle count will determine what days are labeled Buy and what days are labeled Sell or Short Sale.

In designing the LSS system, therefore, there was a need to rephase the cycle when it got out of synch with the traditional 1-2-3 cycle pattern. What was required was a simple indicator that would tell when the market was changing trend. This indicator is known as the trend momentum indicator. It measures the rate at which the market is rising or falling. That is, when a market rallies, it moves up slowly at first, picks up speed, and then, although still rising, the momentum begins to slow, suggesting that a change indirection is imminent. The trend momentum indicator is a helpful tool in this respect.

The rule for rephasing the cycle when you use the trend momentum indicator is simple: each time the trend momentum indicator changes direction, the cycle is rephased. Rephasing involves going back ten days and taking the lowest low as the new L-day (Buy Day) and then counting ahead, L-day, S-day, SS-day, and so on.

How is the trend momentum indicator calculated? This is the rule: take today's close and subtract the close two days previous. Thus: close on day 3 - close on day 1 = momentum indicator number. The number generated is then compared to the two previous trend momentum numbers. The last number will then have one of three patterns in terms of the previous two as follows:

1. Trend momentum indicator number more positive than two previous trend momentum indicator numbers = UP trend
2. Trend momentum indicator number more positive than one of the previous two numbers but more negative than the other number = SIDEWAYS trend
3. Trend momentum indicator number more negative than two previous trend momentum indicator numbers = DOWN trend

Listed below, you will find several consecutive days of closing prices. In the columns to the right, you will find the trend momentum indicator number and the UP, SIDEWAYS, DOWN designation for each. Note that you cannot have a designation until you have at least three trend momentum indicator numbers.

Day	Close	Trend Momentum Indicator #	Trend Momentum Indicator
1	189.25	—	—
2	189.75	—	—
3	187.90	−1.35	—
4	187.40	−2.35	—
5	188.05	+.15	UP
6	188.35	+.95	UP
7	188.45	+.40	SIDEWAYS
8	188.75	+.40	SIDEWAYS
9	187.90	−.55	DOWN

As long as the TMI number is more positive than the two previous numbers, you'll have an UP designation. Note that on day 6, the +.95 is more positive than both +.15 and -2.35—hence the UP designation. But on day 7, the +.40 difference is more negative than day 6 but more positive than day 5—hence the SIDEWAYS designation. Day 8 is considered unchanged, because the +.40 number is not more negative than the previous day's. Lastly, at -.55 on day 9, the designation turns DOWN, because it is more negative than the two previous numbers.

It is important to note that the designation does not determine the direction of the market, only the rate at which it is moving up or down. Look at the close on day 7. The close is higher, but the indicator has turned from UP to SIDEWAYS.

Again, on day 8, the close was higher while the designation was still SIDEWAYS. By day 9, the designation had turned to DOWN and the market had finally turned lower. The indicator tends to lead the market, but it is not used to pinpoint buying or selling opportunities. Rather, the change in the designation signals the rephasing of the cycle.

Often, the cycle will remain the same despite rephasing. For instance, you might have a low that occurred seven or eight days ago, and that designation may have changed several times since then. Each time, you go back and rephase the cycle. In each instance, the lowest low remains the same and the cycle stays intact. In time, however, a new, lower low will be established and the change will indeed change. When this occurs, you base tomorrow's anticipated cycle day on the new rephased day. For instance, let's say that before rephasing, today was designated as a Short Sale Day (SS-day); after rephasing, following today's close, however, today's SS-day becomes an L-day, or Buy Day. Hence, tomorrow's anticipated cycle day is the following day in the cycle, the S-day, or Sell Day.

To see how rephasing might change the three-day cycle, we need to look at an example which is first not rephased, and then, after calculating the trend momentum indicator, in the second example, the cycle is rephased. See how one compares with the other.

Standard & Poor's 500—June 1985

Unrephased Three-day Cycle

Day	Open	High	Low	Close	Indicator Number	Trend
Mar 21 - Thur	182.85	184.55	**182.60	183.20	−.50	DOWN
Mar 22 - Fri	183.45	*183.50	181.95	182.40	−.90	DOWN
Mar 25 - Mon	182.30	*182.40	181.15	181.60	−1.60	DOWN
Mar 26 - Tues	181.70	183.05	*181.40	182.30	−.10	UP
Mar 27 - Wed	182.20	**183.85	181.95	183.10	+1.50	UP
Mar 28 - Thur	183.35	*184.20	182.50	182.80	+.50	SIDEWAYS
Mar 29 - Fri	183.45	183.55	*182.65	183.35	+.25	DOWN
Apr 01 - Mon	183.70	**184.20	183.00	184.10	+1.30	UP
Apr 02 - Tues	184.00	*184.85	182.60	182.95	−.40	DOWN
Apr 03 - Wed	182.90	183.15	**180.80	181.25	−2.85	DOWN

Note: * indicates highs and lows made first during a trading session
    ** signifies a high or low made last during the trading session

In the unrephased three-day cycle shown above, the L-day, or Buy Day, repeats every third day.

In the unrephased three-day cycle shown above, the L-day, or Buy day, repeats every third day.

Standard & Poor's 500—June 1985

Rephased Three-day Cycle

Day	Open	High	Low	Close	Indicator Number	Trend
Mar 21 - Thur	182.85	184.55	**182.60	183.20	—.50	DOWN
Mar 22 - Fri	183.45	*183.50	181.95	182.40	—.90	DOWN
Mar 25 - Mon	182.30	*182.40	181.15	181.60	—1.60	DOWN
Mar 26 - Tues	181.70	183.05	*181.40	182.30	—.10	UP
Mar 27 - Wed	182.20	**183.85	181.95	183.10	+1.50	UP
Mar 28 - Thur	183.35	*184.20	182.50	182.80	+.50	SIDEWAYS
Mar 29 - Fri	183.45	183.55	*182.65	183.35	+.25	DOWN
Apr 01 - Mon	183.70	184.20	*183.00	184.10	+1.30	UP
Apr 02 - Tues	184.00	184.85	**182.60	182.95	—.40	DOWN
Apr 03 - Wed	182.90	*183.15	180.80	181.25	—2.85	DOWN

Note: * signifies a high or low made first during a trading session
** indicates that the high or low was made last during a session

The cycle is rephased each time the momentum trend indicator changes in the second rephased version. (Note: for the days shown, the lowest low occurred on Monday, March 18, at 180.00, the L-day). As a result, the cycle remained intact on the close on March 26. Again, on March 29, the rephased cycle remained intact. The cycle was rephased again on Tuesday, March 26, when the momentum indicator changed from DOWN to UP. New rephasing then occurred on Friday, March 29, and Monday, April 1, and Tuesday, April 2. On each day, the dropping of the day ten days back resulted in a new L-day, or Buy Day, and a new three-day cycle. On Wednesday, April 3, the cycle was not rephased, because the Trend remained DOWN.

The rephasing attempts to relocate the three-day cycle when the highs and lows don't occur as expected. Very often, a simple technique to find the "correct" cycle is to push it ahead one day. For example, let's say today is the SS-day, and the pattern to expect is high made first and then lower prices. But let's say you have the L-day pattern occurring, low made first followed by higher prices. By pushing the cycle ahead one day, you can often find the pattern you are looking for. This, by the way, is one reason why you shouldn't give up when selling into a rally in hopes of capturing a down move. Let's say the market rallies on you and prices move higher. You must take the loss. But chances are, you were simply a day too early. Sell the next day in anticipation of capturing the SS-day high-to-low pattern. You'll find that this works even in bull markets.

Once you find the correct pattern, you can expect two or three cycles of winning trades.

Look at the SS-day that occurred on Monday, March 25. You go in expecting a nice break and sell right at the open. Prices are up a mere .10 points over the open, and down they go. It would be hard to lose by selling short on such a day. Since the pattern seemed reliable at that point, it makes sense to stay with the three-day cycle. The next day, the L-day, you expect the reverse: low made first and rallying prices. You buy at the open or—ideally—a reaction down from the open. Sure enough, March 26 proved an excellent day to buy, since the market rallied off the low early in the day.

Once the market goes into one of its rephasing stages, it often pays to stand aside for three or four days until it finds the cycle once again. Consider, for a moment, what happens when a market breaks. You will have day after day of successive lows. As a result, each time the cycle is rephased, today's new low becomes the Buy day, or L-day. This leaves the least reliable day, in terms of its market direction, the S-day, as the following day. Sooner or later, the actual low—the Buy day low—will occur, and then, typically, the three-day cycle will again become evident. Consider the following table of prices and you'll see why standing aside when the market is rephasing often makes sense.

Standard & Poor's 500—June 1985

Rephased Three-day Cycle

Day	Open	High	Low	Close	Indicator Number	Trend
May 23 · Thur	189.20	*189.60	188.55	188.75	−1.15	DOWN
May 24 · Fri	189.05	**189.40	188.85	189.25	−.10	UP
May 27 · Mon			HOLIDAY			
May 28 · Tues	189.90	190.25	**187.60	188.10	−.65	SIDEWAYS
May 29 · Wed	187.85	188.60	*187.50	188.45	−.80	DOWN
May 30 · Thur	188.25	188.90	*187.40	188.40	+.30	UP
May 31 · Fri	188.25	**190.55	188.05	189.65	+1.20	UP
Jun 03 · Mon	190.85	*190.90	189.30	190.10	+1.70	UP
Jun 04 · Tues	190.20	190.75	*189.65	190.30	+.65	DOWN
Jun 05 · Wed	190.75	*191.15	189.85	189.95	−.15	DOWN

Right after the Memorial Day holiday, the market became rather choppy and the cycle was thrown out of synch. First, the L-day low made first on Tuesday, May 28, failed. Instead, the SS-day pattern—high to low—occurred. Here you could have pushed the cycle ahead a day. There was the L-day pattern the following day, Wednesday, May 29. But the momentum trend indicator, which had been quite choppy, going from DOWN to UP to SIDEWAYS to DOWN in four consecutive days, pinpointed Thursday, May 30, as the S-day, or Sell Day. It was wrong. After rephasing on May 30, the real Buy Day, when the low was made first, occurred and the market rose 3.65 points in four days.

You can see the benefit of rephasing. Looking back on the numbers after the cycle has occurred makes the selection of the Buy Day low an easy one. The problem, however, is spotting the Buy Day low at the same time it is occurring. This particular cycle was a difficult one to find. At the real ten-day low, on Thursday, May 30, most traders were probably selling. Why? Because the market sold off. 85 points from the open and took out the two previous lows by two and four ticks, respectively. This is not an accident. What happened was that a great many traders who, in retrospect, had indeed seen the bottom coming, had the misfortune to place their stops right under the market. So they were right—but wrong! The market was driven down to get the stops—and only then did it soar upward! Note how, after the close, the market received an UP designation. The upward move carried all the way to 191.95 on Friday, June 7.

In summary, the LSS 3-day Cycle Method rephases each time the momentum trend indicator changes designations. Rephasing serves to help you find the correct three-day cycle. In addition, when the anticipated day's pattern doesn't occur as expected, it often pays to push the cycle ahead one day. Remember, there's no rule you have to buy on a so-called L-day or sell short on an SS-day. The names or the days are simply to help you identify the pattern.

CALCULATING THE ENVELOPES

Now that we've covered the discovery of the three-day cycle pattern and discussed the rephasing of the three-day cycle, it is time to identify support and resistance. Where do you think the market will stabilize or encounter price resistance?

One method that has proved to be quite effective is to design two separate envelopes for each trading day. There is a buying envelope, where support can be anticipated, and a selling envelope, where you should expect resistance. As a rule, it is exceedingly difficult to forecast tomorrow's high or low before the market opens. Computer studies have shown that this, and other systems, can occasionally approximate these areas, but, in general, this kind of forecasting method doesn't lend itself to picking two or three key numbers.

What can be accomplished, however, with a high degree of accuracy is the identification of trading zones within which support and resistance should occur. Moreover, once the market is open and you have new data to work

with, the range of these two zones—namely, the buying and selling envelopes—can often be highly accurate, often within one or two ticks.

Let's begin with the buy envelope. What constitutes the buy envelope? As we've defined it, the buy envelope is an area where support should be found in tomorrow's market. Remember, the buy envelope is calculated daily after the close for tomorrow's market. Hence, we only have past data to work with in calculating the numbers. What are the numbers we want to examine? To calculate the buy envelope, we want to look at the following:

1. *The previous day's low*. By previous day, we mean today, the day just finished. If this is Tuesday and the low of the day was 186.00, we want to make note of this number in calculating the buy envelope for Wednesday. Lows are significant because they identify points in the market where the sellers couldn't push prices lower without buyers willingly taking everything the sellers wanted to sell.

2. *The trend reaction buy number*. We have covered the calculation of this number in a previous section. This number represents support.

3. *The average of recent Decline numbers*. Here's where tracking the numbers comes into play. Remember, the Decline column measures the distance between a high and the next day's low. It measures how far a sell-off carried before support was found. As a result, if you could average recent Decline column numbers, and subtract from the previous day's high, you might very well have a ballpark figure on where support could be found. This is where the LSS system has improved Taylor" s original concept. It is important to average recent Decline column entries, because the market can change over time.

4. *The average of recent Buying Under numbers*. The Buying Under number reflects how far under yesterday's low a market carried. If it didn't penetrate the low, the BU number is expressed as a negative number. Again, by averaging the BU entries and subtracting from the previous day's low, you can arrive at a good support level.

The selling envelope is the mirror image of the buying envelope. To calculate the sell envelope, consider the following:

1. *The previous day's high.* In calculating tomorrow's sell envelope, you take today's high as the point where resistance will be encountered. This concept is borrowed from Taylor, who maintained that resistance will always exist at the previous day's high.

2. *The trend reaction sell number.* This number is valuable as a point where resistance will be encountered. The calculation was discussed in an earlier section.

3. *The average of recent Rally numbers.* When added to the previous day's low, the average of the Rally numbers signifies a resistance area where selling should overcome buying.

4. *The average of recent Buying High numbers.* This average is added to the previous day's high. Remember, the BH number is the amount by which the day's high exceeded the previous high. If the last high did not exceed the previous high, the BH number will be negative. By averaging a series of BH numbers, you achieve a consensus that pinpoints a resistance area.

Now, taking both the buy and the sell envelopes, you should have four numbers in each. Since the previous high and low are self-explanatory and the trend reaction numbers have already been discussed, let's look at several examples utilizing the D, R, BH, and BU columns for generating buying and selling numbers for the buy and sell envelopes.

The Decline column. The Decline column measures the range in prices from high to low over a two-day period. Let's consider an actual example in which three consecutive D-column entries were averaged and subtracted from the previous day's high.

First, the target day, which, in our illustration here, we'll assume has yet to take place, Is Thursday, January 10. The most recent data, therefore, are for the previous Monday through Wednesday. The Decline column entries for those three days were as follows:

DAY	DECLINE COLUMN
1	.40
2	1.90
3	.50

The average of these three entries is about .95 points after rounding. You then take the previous day's high and subtract the average of the previous three Decline columns to arrive at a number you can use in the buying envelope. The previous day's high was 169.15. By subtracting .95 points, you arrive at a support level of precisely 168.20. Now remember, this calculation was made following the close on Wednesday, January 9. The previous day's low? Precisely 168.20. Right on the money! Obviously, this was only a coincidence. The likelihood of selecting the exact low using this method is not that great. What's more, once you factor in the other numbers in the envelope, the overall buy number would have been somewhat lower. But this does illustrate how recent price behavior tends to suggest how the market might trade in the near future.

The Buying Under column. Buying Under measures the penetration of the previous day's low. How far under the previous low did the market trade? Obviously, if no penetration occurred, the number would have to be negative, since you will be subtracting a larger number from a smaller one. On Wednesday, January 9, the low of the March S&P contract was 167.10. The previous day's low was 166.35, hence the BU entry will be -.75. The two previous entries were +.60 and -. 95. Here are the three BU entries in column form:

DAY	BUYING UNDER COLUMN
1	-.95
2	.60
3	-.75

The average of the last three entries, therefore, is minus .35 points when averaged. When you subtract a negative number from a number, you add. Therefore, the previous low at 167.10 plus .35 points equals 167.45. This is the entry in the buy envelope as the Buying Under number. As we indicated above, the low on the following target day was 168.20—so this number was a bit low.

The reaction trend number. The reaction trend buy and sell number is derived from the formula provided earlier in the book. The high, low, and close for the day just finished were 169.15, 167.10, and 168.60 respectively. Add them up and divide by three to derive the average; then multiply by two. Subtract the high of 169.15 and obtain the reaction trend buy number, 167.45.

The buy number. The buy number is the average of the four numbers in the buy envelope. The four numbers in, the example we've just covered are as follows:

BUY ENVELOPE

D-column number = 168.20
Reaction number = 167.45
BU-column number = 167.45
Previous low = 167.10
Average of four = 167.55 buy numbers

Now that you know how to derive the buy number, you must know one other rule: you don't buy at the buy number. Rather, the buy and sell numbers are best used to calculate the anticipated range, which we will describe in a moment, as soon as we cover the sell envelope.

The Rally column. The Rally column measures the difference between yesterday's low and today's high, or the range from low to high over the past two-day period. By averaging the magnitude of the rallies, you attempt to anticipate resistance in the market.

Using the data for the March S&P contract for the three days of January 7, 8, and 9, we find that the numbers were as follows:

DAY	RALLY COLUMN
1	2.25
2	.65
3	2.80

The average of these three entries was 1.90 points. When added to the low of the last day of

trading—namely, January 9—the Rally column sell number is 169.00. Indeed, the market on the subsequent day carried far above that number—the top occurred at 172.15. But this number, like the others, only suggests where resistance should occur—not where one should necessarily sell. This is an important point to keep in mind.

The Buying High column. The Buying High column measures the penetration of the last high over the previous high. In the example we are considering, the penetration occurred during the last two out of three sessions. Hence, a negative number was entered on one session. Here's what the columns looked like.

DAY	BUYING HIGH COLUMN
1	.90
2	-.65
3	1.55

The average of the three is, therefore, .60 points. When added to the previous day's high of 169.15, the BH-column entry is 169.75.

The reaction trend number. This is the same formula you used to derive the reaction trend buy number. The only difference is that you subtract the previous low to achieve the sell number. If you do the calculations, you'll see that the reaction trend number is 169.50.

The sell number. The sell number is the average of the four numbers in the sell envelope. The four numbers in the example we've just covered are as follows:

BH-column number = 169.75
Reaction number = 169.50
Previous high = 169.15
R-column number = 169.00
Average of four = 169.35 sell number

Here again, you do not use the sell number to sell. Rather, you use both buy and sell numbers to establish the anticipated range.

The anticipated range. The anticipated range is the difference between the buy number and the sell number. In the example above, the buy number was 167.55 and the sell number was 169.35. The anticipated range, therefore, is the difference between the two, or 1.80 points. The anticipated range is used to pinpoint profit-taking points once an intraday high or low is established.

There are two ways the anticipated range can be used. In the first, you await the establishment of an intraday high or low and then you add or subtract the anticipated range in order to project a high or low for the day. This high or low is known as the target sell or target buy respectively. Quite often, this method is very accurate in predicting the high or low of the day.

For example, let's consider an actual trading situation. For Thursday, January 17, 1985, an L-day with a DOWN designation, the anticipated range of the March 1985 S&P 500 contract was 1.60 points. The buy number was 172.55 and the sell number was 174.15. On Thursday's open, at 173.80, the market rallied two ticks, to 173.90. This was the intraday high. By taking the intraday high and subtracting the anticipated range, you reach a target buy (cover) number of 172.35 (173.90— 1.55 = 172.35). The actual low of the day proved to be 172.15. On the close, the market rallied to 172.60.

Another way to use the anticipated range is to double the number and then add to the low or subtract from the high, depending upon your initial position. In designing the LSS system, many variables were tested as profit-taking points. At first, the testing concentrated on generating many, many winners. To achieve this high probability of winning, small profits were taken—starting with just 50 percent of the range as the target buy or sell. But this soon proved to have its drawbacks. For instance, if you take just 50 percent of the anticipated range and add it to the low or subtract it from the high, you will surely increase the number of times the anticipated range number is reached. After all, if the anticipated range is one point, isn't there a higher likelihood that the market will mount at least a half-point move? Certainly. But the enhanced number of profits will be offset by the inevitable occasional losses, a half-point profit offset by a half point loss. What's more, by taking just 50 percent of the anticipated range, you will find you often leave too many dollars on the table. After many tests, the results proved that doubling the anticipated range maximized the profitability. The reason: on those occasional days when the market really runs, the system will capture the entire move. More often than not, the doubling of the anticipated range means the target buy or sell number is not hit. Since the LSS system is designed for day trading only, you must then exit your position on the close. Typically, this is best achieved by using a market on close (MOC) order.

The advisability of doubling the range is shown by an example. On February 13, 1985, the March S&P contract had an anticipated range of 2.05 points. On the opening, which turned out to be the low of the day, the market mounted a rally. By doubling the anticipated range and adding it to the low of 181.35, a target sell number of 185.45 was established. The actual high of the day proved to be 185.55, just two ticks above the anticipated sell number. The range on the day was over four points—almost double the typical range for the time period. How did the system correctly anticipate the move? It didn't. Rather, it simply allowed the trader to capitalize on the occasional move of four or five points when the market really runs. On the following day, the market reverted to its more normal range, about two points.

THE OVERBOUGHT/OVERSOLD INDICATOR

Should you buy or sell? One of the most reliable aspects of the LSS system is a simple overbought/ oversold indicator that pinpoints when prices have advanced just a little too much during any given trading session, suggesting the reverse action on the following day. Like the "Bullish Consensus" percentages, the overbought/oversold indicator pinpoints when either buyers or sellers gain command of the market. And, like contrary-opinion trading, the LSS system tries to capitalize on the situation by trading against the short-term trend.

Thus, when you have a market that begins near the low and rallies, you will have a high reading on the overbought/oversold indicator;

when the market opens near its high and trades lower, a low reading will occur. As a rule, you want to sell high readings in the indicator which measures 70 percent or higher and you want to buy low readings at 30 percent or lower. The reading is taken each day following the close of trading. The reading applies only to the next day's price action.

Here's the formula for the overbought/oversold indicator:

$$\frac{(\text{High - Open}) + (\text{Close - Low})}{2 \times \text{range}} = \text{overbought/oversold indicator percentage}$$

Let's take an example to illustrate how the overbought/oversold indicator works. We'll look at prices after the close on Thursday, June 13, 1985, in the June S&P contract. The prices at the close that day were as follows:

JUNE S&P—THURSDAY, JUNE 13
Open = 187.10
High = 187.60
Low = 185.50
Close = 185.60

To calculate the overbought/oversold percentage reading, we rely on our formula as follows:

$$\frac{(187.60 - 187.10) + (185.60 - 185.50)}{2 \times (187.60 - 185.50)}$$
$$= \frac{.50 + .10}{2(2.10)}$$
$$= \frac{.60}{4.20}$$
$$= 14\%$$

With a low reading of 14 percent, a buying opportunity presents itself on the following day. Note that, on Thursday, the high was made first and the market declined, setting up a buying opportunity as the market closed near its low.

On the following day, the June S&P contract traded down from its open and then rallied toward the close. The prices were as follows:

JUNE S&P—FRIDAY, JUNE 14
Open = 186.50
High = 187.15
Low = 185.70
Close= 187.05

The overbought/oversold indicator can also be used as a confirming signal for the three-day cycle. Remember, we recently discussed the advisability of occasionally pushing the cycle ahead a day when the ideal pattern can't be ascertained. This is the precise scenario that occurred here. Thursday, June 13, was an S-day with declining prices throughout the trading session after the initial morning bulge that occurred on the open. Instead of challenging the highs on the previous day—Taylor's Buy Day— the market had been in retreat for two consecutive days. The selling was overdone and the market was due to start rallying. Instead of the three-day rally pattern that the classical Taylor trader would expect, the market was trending downward. The third day was indeed the next day, the SS-day. Instead of selling into a rally, however, the S&P trader had to shift his thinking 180 degrees and buy the break. Where was a good place to buy? Right where Taylor said there would be support above the previous day's low. The previous day's low was 185.50. The market found support at 185.70 the next day. By using the overbought/oversold indicator together with the three-day cycle, you could have made a very successful and virtually risk-free trade.

The overbought/oversold indicator works equally well when you have a rising market and you are looking to sell. In a recent three-day cycle that occurred during August 1985, the L-day pattern occurred as forecast, moving from a low made first to a high made last, followed by a second rising market on the following S-day. The pattern was ideal for a short sale on the third day.

Here are the prices for the September S&P contract for the S-day, Thursday, August 8:

SEPT. S&P—THURSDAY, AUGUST 8
Open = 188.50
High = 189.45
Low = 188.25
Close= 189.10

The calculations for the overbought/oversold indicator are as follows:

$$\frac{(189.45 - 188.50) + (189.10 - 188.25)}{2 \times 1.20}$$
$$= \frac{1.80}{2.40}$$
$$= 75\%$$

With the overbought/oversold indicator at 75 percent, the market was ripe for a short sale on the following day. Not only was it the third day up in the three-day cycle, but the overbought/oversold indicator percentage was pointing toward lower prices. Taylor's rule to sell near the previous day's high proved right on the money! Here are the results for the following day:

Open = 189.40
High = 189.50
Low = 188.45
Close= 188.70

The 70-30 rule obviously doesn't prove accurate every day. But when used in conjunction with other signals, it is a valuable contribution to selecting the right trend of the day.

There will be many days when the percentage falls between 70 and 30 percent. How do you use the indicator when the percentage is in the middle? When this occurs, the LSS system turns toward another signal. When a balance exists between buyers and sellers, the balance is reflected by stationary or, at least, sideways price movements. The market may be up in the morning and down in the afternoon and close just about unchanged. On such days, the overbought/oversold indicator will reflect this indecision by registering a neutral reading—say, a 50 percent, or even a 45 or 40 percent, reading. Because the lack of market direction provides no clue to subsequent price action, you have to

look elsewhere for a confirming tool that prices are headed higher or lower.

One good place to look is at the price action during the first hour of trading on the following day. The range which is established during this first hour of trading, we call the intraday range. The high and low registered during the first hour are known as the intraday high and the intraday low respectively. All but the most thinly traded futures will have some range after an hour of trading, even if the underlying cash index or commodity is virtually unchanged. So you will have this range to work with. During the first hour on such a day (namely, when the percentage falls between 30 and 70 percent), you should make it a point to stay out of the market. What you are looking for after the first hour is over and the intraday range is established, is a violation of either the intraday high or the intraday low. Once this violation occurs, you want to fade the move and go the other way.

That is, if the intraday high is violated, look to sell; if the intraday low is violated, look to buy. These are very simple rules, but over a year's time they will return you thousands of dollars in profits.

You can be sure that this is the exact opposite of what most traders are doing—and this, incidentally, is why it works so well. When the market rallies, for instance, several things happen. One, the stops of the short sellers (who have now become buyers) are hit; this, in turn, generates more buying as the latecomers, who've been watching the market for some clue to direction, decide to jump aboard. More buying. Unfortunately for them, they are too late.

These "engineered" rallies—which are called "sucker rallies"—exist solely to fool the unwary. This is the classic Taylor rally, the very paradox that makes the Taylor Book Method and the LSS system so profitable. Essentially, the market is taken up in order to generate a fresh source of buyers for the sellers to sell to; the reverse, of course, is true on the downside. When you think about it, what better time to move the market around a little bit than when the balance between buyer and seller is almost equal? There is no "reason" for the market to rally, so why not

Standard & Poor's 500—December 1984

Ten Consecutive Trading Days—Level 1 Trades

| | Initiate | | Liquidate | | |
Date	Bought/Sold	Time	Bought/Sold	Time	Gain/Loss
09/05/84	Buy 3 @ 167.70	10:38*	Sell 3 @ 168.10	3:14**	+$ 600
09/06/84			no trade		
09/07/84			no trade		
09/10/84	Buy 3 @ 166.30	9:31	Sell 3 @ 168.40	3:14	+$ 3,150
09/11/84	Sell 3 @ 169.35	9:02	Buy 3 @ 167.05	3:14	+$ 3,450
09/12/84	Buy 3 @ 167.15	9:04	Sell 3 @ 168.35	3:14	+$ 1,800
09/13/84	Sell 3 @ 169.30	12:21	Buy 3 @ 169.70	12:55	−$ 600
09/14/84	Sell 3 @ 174.40	9:11	Buy 3 @ 172.75	3:14	+$ 2,475
09/17/84	Buy 3 @ 172.25	9:03	Sell 3 @ 172.95	3:14	+$ 1,050
09/18/84			no trade		
09/19/84	Buy 3 @ 172.10	9:01	Sell 3 @ 174.30	1:09	+$ 3,300
09/20/84	Buy 3 @ 170.65	9:20	Sell 3 @ 171.55	3:14	+$ 1,350
09/21/84	Sell 3 @ 170.80	9:03	Buy 3 @ 170.50	2:11	+$ 450

Total Profits: $17,025

* central daylight saving time
** 3:14 signifies MOC order

create a modest "technical rally" to get the ball rolling?

There could be a million and one excuses that will be credited for the false rally—the Fed was loosening credit, rumors of tight crop, or whatever—but you can be sure that, regardless of the reason, the smart money will profit and the uninformed will lose.

There is a reason, of course. But not the one you'll find broadcast on the TV or radio news. The reason is that the insiders wanted to create a good selling opportunity, and they could accomplish this feat only by panicking the hapless short sellers into buying at an unadvantageous price. You have to remind yourself that there's always a buyer for each seller, and vice versa. Typically, those who engineer the early-morning false breakout know exactly what they are doing. Join their ranks and see how profitable it can be.

USING THE OPENING PRICE TO BUY OR SELL—THE LEVEL I TRADE

Statistical studies have shown that the opening and closing prices are often near one end of the day's range. Typically, the opening will fall near one end of the range and the close near the other. This is not to suggest that the key to beating the market is to simply buy on the open and sell on the close, however.

The LSS system relies on using three levels of prices to initiate positions. One of these levels, which is known as Level 1, relies on buying or selling at a fixed variable, away from the morning's opening price. For obvious reasons, the variable will be different for different futures contracts. The volatility of the market, the size of the daily range, and the market's tendency to retrace its initial intraday range will all determine what the variable should be.

two key functions. On the one hand, a move of x points away from the open suggests the market is experiencing normal volatility and it may again soon reverse its direction; on the other hand, a larger move, of y points, in the same direction means that a reversal is highly unlikely.

Let's look at this idea in terms of an actual market experience.

Several years ago, when moves of $20 and even limit moves of $25 an ounce were not uncommon in gold, I learned an interesting statistic. A trader who had run tests on the gold market told me that if gold prices were headed lower, the rise from the opening price would exceed $3 only 30 percent of the time and that it would exceed $4 only 12 percent of the time. That meant that if gold was going to trade lower

on any given day, it would not rise above $4 over the opening price 88 percent of the time. I took this to mean that I could safely sell gold on a rally from the open and place a relatively close stop to protect my position. As prices gathered strength and rose about a $4.00 premium over the opening price, I would then take losses on any short position and look for an opportunity to begin purchasing gold futures contracts. It wasn't long before I realized precisely what valuable information this was. When buying, I would wait for a decline in prices under the open. If, for example, gold opened at $570 an ounce, I would often buy it at $567 and watch the market. If it went more than a dollar or two against me, I promptly got out. More often than not, however, the market found support at the

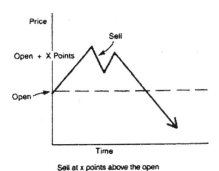

Sell at x points above the open

Figure 53.   The Level 1 Sell Trade.

Standard & Poor's 500—December 1984

Ten Consecutive Trading Days—Level 2 Trades

Date	Initiate Bought/Sold	Time	Liquidate Bought/Sold	Time	Gain/Loss
09/05/84	Buy 3 @ 168.05	10:04*	Sell 3 @ 168.10	3:14**	+$ 75
09/06/84			no trade		
09/07/84			no trade		
09/10/84	Buy 3 @ 166.45	10:11	Sell 3 @ 168.40	3:14	+$ 2,925
09/11/84	Sell 3 @ 169.50	10:07	Buy 3 @ 167.05	3:14	+$ 3,675
09/12/84	Buy 3 @ 167.45	1:59	Sell 3 @ 168.35	3:14	+$ 1,350
09/13/84	Sell 3 @ 168.75	12:11	Buy 3 @ 169.70	12:55	−$ 1,425
09/14/84	Sell 3 @ 174.05	10:00	Buy 3 @ 172.75	3:14	+$ 1,950
09/17/84	Buy 3 @ 172.60	10:19	Sell 3 @ 172.95	3:14	+$ 525
09/18/84			no trade		
09/19/84	Buy 3 @ 172.05	10:00	Sell 3 @ 174.30	1:09	+$ 3,375
09/20/84	Buy 3 @ 170.85	11:16	Sell 3 @ 171.55	3:14	+$ 1,050
09/21/84	Sell 3 @ 171.90	11:53	Buy 3 @ 170.50	2:11	+$ 2,100

Total Profits: $15,600

* central daylight saving time
** 3:14 signifies MOC order

level and rallied, generating profits.

In the Standard & Poor's 500 index contract, extensive computer tests revealed that the same type of pattern was evident. The market could easily move x points away from the open if it was headed in the reverse direction; but once it went y points, that was the direction in which it would likely trend—not, however, necessarily right away. At first, during the early volatility of the contract, .40 or .50 points seemed the ideal spot to place an entry order away from the open. But as more data became available, .30 points above the open when selling, or .30 points below the open when buying, became the logical entry point. For one, using a smaller variable when entering will get you into more positions. For another, over time this greater number of positions tends to enhance your profits.

It is important to note that these so-called Level I trades will be taken as soon as you have some clue as to market direction—that is, as soon after the open as possible, in most instances. In many cases, the opportunity to buy .30 points under the open or .30 points above the opening on days in which you have selected the correct direction, may exist for only a moment. For this reason, you must be quick to enter your order as soon as the opening price is known. Figures 53 and 54 illustrate the Level I trade.

Let's look at ten consecutive trading days in which you are buying or selling at the .30 point variable above or below the open. These are actual trades that have been verified by computer. When the position was stopped out, the table indicates by showing a loss in the position.

For the ten days shown, the Level I buying/selling strategy returned an average of $1,672.50 per day using just three contracts on each trade. You should note that, for the thirteen trading days, three days had no Level I trade. This is because the market did not trade up .30 from the open on selling or down .30 points from the open on buying. On some days, how-ever, no trade, either buying or selling, is indicated and the LSS system calls for standing on the sidelines.

Eight out of the nine trades were taken during the first thirty-one minutes of trading. Seven out of ten trades were exited on the close using a market-on-close order. One trade was stopped out with a loss. Significantly, this trade was taken relatively late in the day and was stopped out after only thirty-four minutes. In the two other examples, the profit point was reached. This illustrates the importance of placing orders early in the day, preferably right after the open, when the day's market direction is unknown, and exiting late in the day, preferably on the close.

The open is often the best time of day to initiate trades. You'd do well to watch the open carefully and enter your orders as soon after the opening price is known as possible.

THE RETRACEMENT OF THE INTRADAY RANGE—THE LEVEL 2 TRADE

Known as the Level 2 trade, the retracement trade is based on the tendency of a market to mount a countertrend before taking its natural upward or downward course during the day. The intraday range is defined in the LSS system as the range of prices after one hour of trading. The retracement trade price is determined by taking the intraday range and multiplying the range by .618. The resultant product is then added to the intraday low when buying or subtracted from the intraday high when selling. (See Figures 55 and 56.)

For example, on November 1, 1984, the intraday high and the intraday low for the December 1984 S&P 500 contract was 169.85 and 169.30. The intraday range was the difference between the numbers, or .55 points. Multiplying by .618, the result is .35 points. This amount is then subtracted from the intraday high to achieve the Level 2 buying price at 169.55. The market indeed traded at that price and three contracts were purchased at a price of 169.55. They were sold on the close at 170.45, resulting in a profit of $1,350 for the day. The maximum adversity on this trade was very little, since the low of the day was only .30 points below the entry point.

In the following table, we have listed ten consecutive trading days of Level 2 trades.

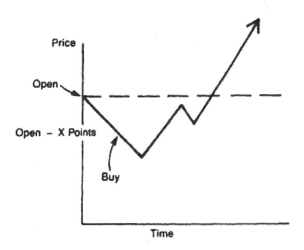

Buy at x points below the open

Figure 54. The Level 1 Buy Trade.

The profits on the Level 2 trades almost mirror those on the Level I trades for the same time period. The profits are a little less: $15,600 as compared to $16,725. But they are still quite respectable.

You should note that no Level 2 trades are ever taken during the first hour of trading. By definition, a Level 2 trade can be taken only after the intraday high and the intraday low are established.

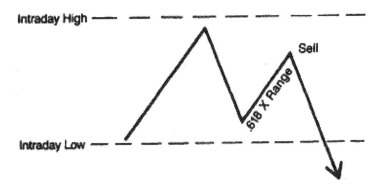

Figure 55. The Retracement Sell.

THE PENETRATION OF THE INTRADAY HIGH OR LOW—THE LEVEL 3 TRADE

The Level 3 trade is taken only when the intraday high or the intraday low is penetrated by a given amount. When selling, the Level 3 trade is taken upon the violation of the Intraday high. When buying, the Level 3 trade is taken upon the violation of the intraday low. The variable to use in determining the amount of penetration in placing the buying or selling price of the Level 3 trade is 15 percent of the day's anticipated range. Thus, if the anticipated range in the Standard & Poor's contract is 2.00 points, the penetration number will be .30 points above the intraday high (if selling) or .30 points below the intraday low (if buying). Figures 57 and 58 illustrate the Level 3 buy and sell trade.

Let's consider an example. On July 6, 1984, the anticipated range for the September 1984 S&P contract was 1.50 points. Fifteen percent of this amount is 22.5, so we'll round the penetration number to .25 points. The intraday high was 154.10 and the intraday low was 153.70. Since we are buying on this day, we would place an order to purchase September S&P contracts at a price of 153.45 after one hour of trading.

At precisely 10:11 that morning, just eleven minutes after the establishment of the intraday range, three contracts were purchased at that price. They were sold at the close at 154.15. The profit: $1,050. Because Level 3 trades are only taken upon a penetration of the Intraday high or the intraday low, there are far fewer of them than of the Level I and Level 2 intraday High trades. The Level 3 trades tend to be the most profitable. This is because they are placed at the highest price when selling and the lowest when buying. For this reason, the Level 3 trade is a difficult one to take for most traders. Typically, the stops are being run at the time the position is initiated and you are selling strength or buying

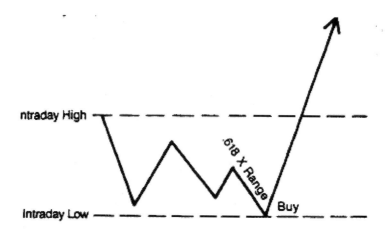

Figure 56. The Retracement Buy.

weakness.

In the table below, you will find listed the Level 3 trades for the ten consecutive trading days shown in the previous tables. Note that there are only two trades—and only one winner.

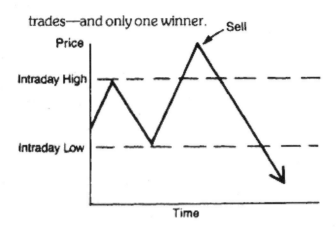

Figure 57. The Level 3 Sell Trade.

Standard & Poor's 500—December 1984

Ten Consecutive Trading Days—Level 3 Trades

Date	Initiate Bought/Sold	Time	Liquidate Bought/Sold	Time	Gain/Loss
09/05/84			no Level 3 trade		
09/06/84			no trade		
09/07/84			no trade		
09/10/84			no Level 3 trade		
09/11/84			no Level 3 trade		
09/12/84			no Level 3 trade		
09/13/84	Sell 3 @ 169.25	12:23*	Buy 3 @ 169.70	12:55	−$ 675
09/14/84			no Level 3 trade		
09/17/84			no Level 3 trade		
09/18/84			no trade		
09/19/84			no Level 3 trade		
09/20/84			no Level 3 trade		
09/21/84	Sell 3 @ 173.15	10:20	Buy 3 @ 170.50	2:11	+$ 3,975

Total Profits: $3,300

* central daylight saving time

For the ten days on which trades occurred, the LSS system gained over $35,000 when the three trading levels are taken together. On only two of these days would a maximum of nine contracts have been traded.

THE LSS WORKSHEET

At the heart of the LSS system is the worksheet. Comparable to Taylor's Book Method, the worksheet contains all the important data you'll need to calculate the buying and selling envelopes, the cycle, the overbought/oversold, the trend, and the rallies and declines—in short, everything you'll need to trade the LSS system effectively and profitably.

Purchasers of the LSS software will find that much of the calculating is performed by their personal computer. The only requirement for PC users is to enter the daily price data as well as answer the questions requested by the program. To provide the correct trading signals, the software program will require you to enter the morning's opening as well as the intraday high and the intraday low. Once this information is known, however, the software will do the rest.

The LSS trading system is also available in the form of a Hewlett-Packard 41 hand-held calculator that has been preprogrammed. Here again, the user will be responsible for entering correct price data and answering the respective questions concerning opening price and intraday high and low. The calculator will then perform all the mathematical calculations associated with generating the trading signals.

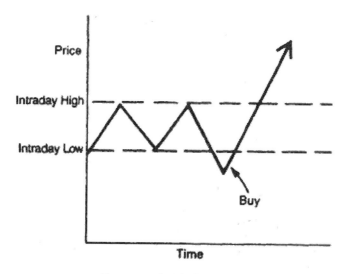

Buy at x points below the intraday high

Figure 58. The Level 3 Buy Trade.

For users who would prefer to do all the calculations manually, the accompanying worksheet should provide a guideline. Note that the open, high, low, and close are entered every day. Once this information is available, you can then enter the momentum trend number and the momentum trend indicator.

The overbought/oversold percentage can also be calculated from these numbers, as can the trend reaction numbers and the Decline, Rally Buying High, and Buying Under numbers. Finally, the buy and sell envelopes and the respective buy and sell numbers can be calculated.

It is important to track this vital market information daily. Unless the price data are entered daily, the correct trading cycle will be lost, as will be other important information.

Even a cursory glance at the table following should help you immediately make some

128

decisions for the next trading day, Friday, June 14. One would anticipate the next day's cycle day as an SS-day, or the third day in the three-day pattern with the normal SS-day cycle pattern of high made first and low made last. But, in this instance, you can see from the overbought/oversold indicator that the 14 percent reading suggests the reverse: a buying opportunity on the next day's open.

Here's what happened. The June 1985 S&P 500 contract opened at 186.50. The LSS system immediately signaled a buy at the open minus .30 points, or 186.20. This trade was taken during the first hour of trading.

After one hour of trading, the intraday high and the intraday low were known. The intraday high was 186.50, the opening price, and the intraday low was 185.70, which proved to be the low of the day. By taking this intraday range and multiplying by .618 and then subtracting the product from the intraday high, the Level 2 buy signal was generated at 186.00. This price,

however, was never reached again during the trading day. The Level 3 buy signal, which would have been at 185.40 on a penetration of the intraday low, was not hit either.

The positions were sold on a market-on-close order for a profit of $1,275 for the day. The open, high, low, and close were as follows:

S&P 500—June 1985
Friday, June 14
Open = 186.50
High = 187,15
Low 185.70
Close= 187.05

Note also that the trend reaction sell number was 187.00 and the actual high proved to be 187.15. Also, the sell number in the selling envelope was 186.85, just .30 points off the high of the day. By holding the position until the close, however, the LSS system realized a

Standard & Poor's 500

June 1985

Date	Open	High	Low	Close	Ovbt/ Ovsld	T#	T	D	R	BH	BU	Pivot NR	Buy	Sell
June 06 Th	189.75	**191.70	189.55	191.60	93%	+ 1.30	U	1.60	1.85	.55	.30	190.20-B 192.35-S	189.95	191.80
07 F	191.50	191.95	**189.50	189.55	10%	− .40	D	2.20	2.40	.25	.05	188.75-B 191.20-S	189.55	191.75
10 M	189.35	**190.05	188.85	189.95	71%	− 1.75	D	3.10	.55	− 1.90	.65	189.15-B 190.35-S	188.55	190.15
11 T	189.85	*190.05	188.85	189.25	25%	− .30	U	1.20	1.20	0	0	188.75-B 189.95-S	188.50	189.95
12 W	189.20	189.35	**187.65	187.85	10%	− 2.00	D	2.40	.50	− .70	1.20	187.25-B 188.95-S	187.25	188.80
13 Th	187.10	*187.60	185.50	185.60	14%	− 3.65	D	3.85	− .05	− 1.75	2.15	184.90-B 187.00-S	184.95	186.85

Note: *means that the highs and lows were made first during the trading session
**signifies a high or low being achieved last during the trading session

129

slightly better selling price on the day.

Some other observations on the use of the LSS worksheet are shown in the table. The overbought-oversold percentage worked four days out of six. Using this indicator alone would have had you selling on Friday, June 7; buying on Monday, June 10; selling on Tuesday, June 11; and buying on Friday, June 14. These were all winning trades. Moreover, using the Level I trades alone, the maximum adversity from the entry point would have been remarkably small.

For instance, on Friday, June 7, you would have sold the Level 1 position at 191.80, and the high of the day proved to be 191.95, three ticks higher. On Monday, June 10, the Level I buy occurred at 189.05, and the bottom was 188.85, four ticks away. On Tuesday, June 11, the Level I trade was missed by just two ticks (although the Level 2 trade would have proved profitable); and, finally, the winning trade on Friday, June 14, would have been taken at 186.20, resulting in a maximum adversity of .50 points prior to the move into profitability. Note also that the Level 1 sell on Friday, June 7, was confirmed by the selling number (191.80) being at the same exact price. The profit on the Level I trade on that day was $3,375 using just three contracts.

HOW PROFITABLE IS THE LSS SYSTEM?

The LSS system was tested by obtaining the tick-by-tick data available from the Chicago Mercantile Exchange and then running the computerized LSS program against the data. It is important to note that the computer looked at every tick of every day in doing its analysis of how the system would work under actual market conditions. Most computerized systems, by contrast, are tested only against high, low, close data, which is far less accurate as a testing model. What's more, actual real-time testing with real dollars in the market since the development of the system suggests that the computerized simulation tracks the real-time record closely.

As a day-trading method, the LSS system carries no positions overnight. All the profits and losses that occur in the system are realized on a single-day basis. Stops are used every day, and losses are never allowed to overwhelm the user. As a result, the system adheres to the well-known dictum to "cut your losses and let your profits ride." Whenever the profit-taking point is not reached, all positions are liquidated with a market-on-close order.

The system was tested on one period of time and then run against a significantly longer period. All the testing occurred in the most active month of the Standard & Poor's 500 contract. The LSS system may very well work equally as well or better on a number of other futures contracts, but there are difficulties in obtaining data to test other contracts. For example, none of the New York exchanges had tick-by-tick data available. Much of the data available at the Chicago Board of Trade were incomplete or downright inaccurate. As a result, Chicago testing was limited to the S&P 500 and other futures traded at the Merc. However, the introduction of new stock index contracts, which haven't traded long enough to have price data histories, should prove good candidates for the LSS 3-day Cycle Method.

Now let's turn toward results. Over a thirty-two-month period, the LSS system, using just three contracts at each of the three price levels, returned a gross profit of $408,075.50. This was on a purely mechanical basis, taking the trades and using the stops and profit points just as has been spelled out in this chapter. During this period, the market had trended both up and down as well as sideways. The maximum drawdown averaged just 12 percent, a healthy number by almost any standard, and the so-called Shape Ratio, by which many analysts judge a system, was 3.89. A reading of 2.00 or higher is considered a good ratio for most systems. About half of all trades resulted in profits. Significantly, the average profit was much higher than the average loss.

RULES FOR THE LSS SYSTEM

The LSS system is a mechanical day-trading method that does not require interpretation or judgments during market hours. Because it attempts to capture a single move during a trading session, the system works best on volatile futures such as the stock indexes or the currencies. Despite its mechanical nature, however, the LSS system can be improved by employing certain judgments and intuitive reasoning. The rules that follow can help you trade the system successfully.

RULE NUMBER 1. *Track the cycle every day.* To use the LSS system, you must keep track of the daily price data and the three-day cycle. This also involves doing the calculations every day. Without the calculations and the phasing of the cycle, you cannot determine the anticipated range or other essential measurements for trading the system. Fortunately, the math is relatively simple. But the trader must be willing to put in the time to follow the market on a day-to-day basis. The software or an HP-41 preprogrammed calculator can help make this task easier.

RULE NUMBER 2. *Minimize commission costs.* With the trend toward discount brokerage services, this shouldn't be a hard rule to follow. Moreover, it makes sense. Why pay two or three times as much in commissions when you can get the same service without paying the higher fees of many brokerage houses? The LSS system generates, on average, about ninety to a hundred trades a month. This translates into more than a thousand round-turn trades a year. A savings of even one dollar per trade, therefore, will result in another thousand dollars in profits that you'll have to keep.

As a rule, you shouldn't have to pay more than $20 per round-turn at today's rates. And, depending on the size of your account and the volume, you should be able to negotiate a significantly lower commission.

An alternative to discount brokerage for the serious trader is to purchase a membership on one of the commodity exchanges. If you become a member, your costs will fall significantly. Depending on whether you trade for your account on the floor of the exchange or over the phone through a broker, your cost as a member will be as low as one dollar per trade or as high as $4.00 or $5.00—still a significant savings below the rates charged to public traders.

RULE NUMBER 3. *Act on the trading signals.* The system won't help you unless you learn to take the trades as they occur. The best trades, unfortunately, rarely present themselves for a long period of time. Typically, the best price of the day occurs shortly after the open. The system is designed to help you find this trade. But unless you have the quick-wittedness to place the order without hesitation, the market will likely get away from you, and your only alternative will be to chase the market—a risky strategy at best.

The serious money in the futures market is made by those fortunate traders who aren't afraid to fade the short-term trend. Trust the signals and place your orders before the prices are hit. In this manner, your order will be filled and you'll be earning profits right from the start.

RULE NUMBER 4. *Pay attention to the buy and sell numbers and envelopes.* Although the buying and selling levels are clearly spelled out in the LSS system, the serious trader can enhance his trading skills by watching for key support and resistance areas within the buy envelopes and sell envelopes respectively. When the numbers in both the buying envelopes and selling envelopes match those of the three levels generated by the system, the trade is apt to be a good one. What's more, once the key support or resistance is broken by having prices fall out of the bottom of the buy envelope or soar out of the top of the selling envelope, the trend is likely to persist. At this point, you might do well to use a stop-and-reverse order. Some traders make it a policy to double up and reverse when their position is stopped out. But you must be careful where you do this. Typically, the best opportunities for reversing occur early in the day. A violation of the buy envelope or sell envelope is often a sign that the trend is going in the direction of the penetration of the envelope.

RULE NUMBER 5. *Don't be afraid to take losses quickly when you are wrong.* Good trades tend to go your way almost from the very start. Bad trades, on the other hand, have a way of going against you and staying that way. It won't hurt to take a loss and then try to take the same position later if the situation warrants. Otherwise, you run the risk of burying yourself and overstaying a losing trade. This is not to suggest that you shouldn't add to a loser. Under some circumstances, you want to take another trade when the stops are being run against you. Typically, despite the temporary adversity, the market will soon begin to move in your favor. But once you get behind and the market doesn't seem to want to go your way, you should be willing to take the loss and get out of the market. Never, never hold a losing—or winning—position overnight. You could take an occasional winner overnight, but never a loser. There's a reason why day trading is attractive: safety. Don't attempt to second-guess the market by staying overnight. You are only inviting trouble when you hold on to losing trades.

RULE NUMBER 6. *Don 't trade too many different commodities or financial futures.* The LSS system was designed primarily with the Standard & Poor's 500 contract in mind. It is unlikely that it will work as well with other futures contracts, although there is some evidence that it has a good track record in the pork belly market and the soybean market. One reason for good profitability is high volatility. Unless you are in a market that moves, you are going to have trouble making significant profits. What's more, by following too many markets, you are likely to miss an occasional trade. Good trading requires concentration. The closer you follow one or two markets, the better your trading will be.

RULE NUMBER 7. *When the cycle seems out of synch, push it ahead a day.* The rephasing is designed to help you find the correct cycle as quickly as possible. But a simple rule is to look for the reverse to occur on the following day. For example, if you are looking to sell today with the high made first and the low last, and

the reverse occurs, look for the selling pattern tomorrow. After all, now you have the market rising and the longs will have profits. To take those profits, they will need to sell.

Typically, the larger traders prefer selling into rallies. The morning bulge on the opening on the next day typically signals the imminent break in prices. For buying opportunities, of course, the reverse is true.

Current Publications of Traders Press

12 Habitudes of Highly Successful Traders.........	Roosevelt
A Comparison of 12 Technical Trading Systems	Brorsen & Lukac
A Complete Guide to Trading Profits..................	Paris
A Professional Look at S & P Day Trading..........	Trivette
A Treasury of Wall Street Wisdom......................	Coslow & Schultz
Ask Mr. Easy Language.......................................	Tennis
Astro-Cycles: The Trader's Viewpoint................	Pesavento
Channels and Cycles: A Tribute to J.M. Hurst....	Millard
Chart Reading for Professional Traders.............	Jenkins
Cyclic Analysis: A Dynamic Approach to T.A.....	Hurst
Dynamic Trading..	Miner
Essentials of Trading..	Jouflas & Pesavento
Exceptional Trading: The Mind Game................	Roosevelt
Fibonacci Ratios with Pattern Recognition........	Pesavento
Futures Spread Trading: The Complete Guide...	Smith
Gann for the Active Trader.................................	Ferrera
Geometry of Stock Market Profits......................	Jenkins
Harmonic Vibrations..	Pesavento
How to Trade in Stocks......................................	Livermore & Smitten
Investing by the Stars...	Weingarten
Investor Skills Training......................................	Ronin
It's Your Option...	Zelkin
Keeping a Cool Head in a Hot Market...............	Roosevelt
Magic of Moving Averages.................................	Lowry
Market Beaters...	Collins
Market Rap...	Collins
Mind Over Markets..	Dalton
Option Strategies for Sophisticated Traders.......	Crask
Overcoming Seven Deadly Sins of Trading.........	Roosevelt
Pit Trading: Do You Have the Right Stuff?........	Bacetti & Hoffman
Planetary Harmonics of Speculative Markets.....	Pesavento
P & F Charting: The Complete Guide.................	Aby
P & F Commodity & Stock Trading Techniques..	Zieg
Precision Trading...	Stevenson
Private Thoughts from a Traders Diary...............	MacKay & Pesavento
Professional Commodity Traders........................	Kroll
Profitable Grain Trading....................................	Ainsworth
Profit Magic of Stock Transaction Timing..........	Hurst
Profitable Patterns for Stock Trading.................	Pesavento
Roadmap to the Markets.....................................	Busby

**Want more information on hundreds of trading titles?
Contact us for a free catalog!**

(800) 927-8222
www.traderspress.com